The Hill Towns of Italy

Skyline, Trevi

The Hill Towns

of

Italy

photographs

BY RICHARD KAUFFMAN

text

BY CAROL FIELD

CHRONICLE BOOKS

SAN FRANCISCO

First Chronicle Books edition 1997.

Library of Congress Cataloging-in-Publication Data:
Kauffman, Richard, 1916–
    The hill towns of Italy / photographs by Richard Kauffman; text
by Carol Field
        p.   cm.
    Originally published: New York: Dutton, 1983.
    Includes index.
    ISBN 0-8118-1354-1
    1. Cities and towns–Italy–Tuscany–History. 2. Cities and
towns–Italy–Umbria–History. 3. Tuscany (Italy)–History, Local.
4. Umbria (Italy)–History, Local. I. Field, Carol. II. Title.
DG736.5.K38 1996
945'.5—dc20
                                      96-2437
                                      CIP

Design and composition by Juliette Robbins.

Printed in Singapore.

Distributed in Canada by Raincoast Books
8680 Cambie Street
Vancouver, B.C. V6P 6M9

10 9 8 7 6 5 4 3 2 1

Chronicle Books
85 Second Street
San Francisco, CA 94105

Web Site: www.chronbooks.com

"Remember," he concluded, "that it is only by going off
the track that you get to know the country. See the little
towns—Gubbio, Pienza, Cortona, San Gimignano . . .
and don't, let me beg of you, go with that awful idea that
Italy's only a museum of antiquities and art."

E. M. FORSTER
Where Angels Fear to Tread

Piazza del Populo, Todi

Umbrian haystack

Contents

Acknowledgments   ix

Notes,
    photographic and otherwise   xi

Introduction   xiii

Map   xvi

A Short History   1

TUSCANY   19   UMBRIA   67

Siena   29   Perugia   73

San Gimignano   37   Assisi   79

Montepulciano   43   Orvieto   89

Pienza   47   Todi   97

Volterra   51   Spoleto   103

Cortona   57   Gubbio   109

Arezzo   61

Index   113

In the Duomo, Perugia

Acknowledgments

This book would not even exist without Barbara and Jack Rosston, wonderful friends who dreamed up the collaboration and brought us together.

During the writing of the book, I was helped immeasurably by many people. In Italy, Gianna and Riccardo Bertelli, Shirley and François Caracciolo, and Ann Cornelisen offered invaluable ideas and information. Paola Bagnatori first taught me the language and has helped in innumerable ways. My thanks go as well to Linda Gunnarson, who was so enthusiastic that she went to live in Tuscany; to Franco Crespi; to Gene Brucker for reading what I had written and saving me from many mistakes; to Peter Davison and Jane in memoriam; to Fred Hill; to Wiley Feinstein; to Amanda Pope and Barry Traub, encouraging and wonderful friends who had a lot to do with the book in its various stages; to my father, James D. Hart, who made many suggestions and brought me endless books; and to Doris Ober, who typed and retyped and was extraordinarily generous with both her time and her help. Most of all, I want to thank my husband, John, who first introduced me to Italy and then took me back to live, and who has been unfailingly supportive over the long period of the book's gestation. Without his support and that of Matthew and Alison, I could never have succeeded.

CAROL FIELD

I would like to express my deep appreciation to my wife, Elinore, my enthusiastic helpmate and delightful companion who returned to Tuscany and Umbria with me year after year for the ten trips devoted to making the photographs for this book.

RICHARD KAUFFMAN

Farmhouse, Umbria

Notes

PHOTOGRAPHIC AND OTHERWISE

Memories of a first trip to the hill towns of Northern Italy taken thirty years ago have brought me back again and again during the last decade to photograph these towns: memories of handsome white oxen standing in the traces of carts in the Piazza del Duomo in San Gimignano; of narrow Spoletan streets winding steeply to the town's crest; of the architectural splendors of the Palazzo dei Consuli in Gubbio and the Torre del Mangia in Siena; of the polychrome façade of the Orvieto Duomo, glowing in the late afternoon sun; and of luminous Umbrian and Tuscan landscapes.

Much had changed when I returned to photograph, though happily much remained. Unfortunately the oxen were gone; the towns were bustling with automobiles. The medieval architecture, on the other hand, was mostly untouched, as was the countryside.

I am a romantic. I delight in the past, in the picturesqueness of a vanishing (or a vanished) civilization. I see bygone days through rose-colored glasses, and like Miniver Cheevy, I miss "the medieval grace of iron clothing." This perception carries over into photography. With my camera, I avoid the roofs bristling with television antennas, the piazzas filled with Fiats (no easy task), and I strive to re-create, as best I can, the hill towns I saw some thirty years ago.

While I have photographed this area primarily for its aesthetic appeal, I do believe that I am addressing another cause—that of conservation. One certainly cannot be against modernization when it improves the human condition, but a mindless destruction of beauty and antiquity, as has been taking place in the larger hill towns, is cause for great concern.

Today, documentary photography is a most popular form of the craft, and deservedly so. Such photography shows our culture in the hard light of fact, tending, because of its reportorial nature, to emphasize the less appealing aspects. Necessary as it may be for social commentary, it is not for me.

While the shock value of depicting a lovely medieval church converted into a garage may marshal public opinion toward a preservationist stance, I believe the same results may be achieved in a more subtle and palatable form—by showing the viewer harmonious images, which persuade him that the best of the past must be saved and that beauty is a precious and fragile commodity.

RICHARD KAUFFMAN

At Santa Chiara, Assisi

Introduction

When this book was first published in 1983, travelers were already finding their way to the hill towns of Tuscany and Umbria, and in the intervening years, more and more of them have discovered Siena and San Gimignano, Assisi, Perugia, and Todi. Ever greater numbers have meandered into the dramatic landscape of southern Tuscany, where Montepulciano and Pienza claim their hillsides, where such abbeys as Sant'Antimo and San Galgano sit in silence in the green countryside. People have driven through the awesome parched geography of rock and stone leading to Volterra, which clings precariously to the edge of steeply eroding cliffs, and have ventured even to tiny Città di Bagnorégio, reached by a narrow bridge of earth across a deep chasm. They have seen tiny hilltop towns rising above golden fields of summer wheat, swaths of dark green tobacco, and wide rivers of yellow sunflowers flowing down valley as far as the eye can see. Drawn by the harmony of the landscape and the continuity of the cultural and architectural fabric, they have succumbed to the beauty of a land where the works of man and nature are so intertwined that it is almost impossible to separate one from the other.

The delights of wandering through the countryside, the impromptu decision to follow an unknown road, to explore a cluster of stone buildings, tower, and fortress and a handful of houses whose terra-cotta roof tiles are spattered with ancient golden lichen: Tuscany and Umbria draw us not only for the great cities and astonishing works of art, but also for the deeply satisfying natural setting, for towns perched high on hills, for the pleasure of finding piazze where old men sit wearing hats beneath the shade of a gigantic tree. The solemnity and silence of many of these cities often make it easy to imagine life in their streets during the Middle Ages, when most took the form by which we know them today. Some, like Gubbio and Pienza, have barely changed; some, like San Gimignano, have new restaurants and shops where artisans purvey their wares to attract the many visitors who come to see the city bristling with its towers. Others, like Siena, have grown and contracted and grown again to the point that it is almost impossible to visualize that city in the nineteenth century, when Hazlitt suggested the slogan "it was" to describe its shrunken state and Taine called it "a Pompeii of the Middle Ages."

Should a visitor arrive on a festival day, as Henry James inadvertently did when he reached Cortona, the experience of a place will be completely different. Exuberant inhabitants fill piazze and narrow, winding

Duomo, Spoleto, sundown

streets that are usually silent and deserted. They may be observing a religious feast, they may be celebrating the glory of the city's past, or they may even be holding a sagra honoring the first fruits of the local fields. One should really go to Spello twice. Once for Corpus Domini in June, when the town is briefly carpeted by brilliant tapestries and paintings that look at first glance as if they might have been painted by Raphael or Michelangelo. Closer examination reveals that these amazing works of art are formed entirely of flower petals arranged in astonishingly subtle gradations of color and complex designs, laid on the paving of the hill town's single uninterrupted street. Crowds serpentine along its edge to see the finished works, and inhabitants of Spello aid them by leaving open their front doors, inviting spectators to climb to higher floors so they can view the designs in their entirety. Come back when the last of the petals have blown away and the city has returned to its more peaceful rhythms and you

will discover a place of irresistible gentleness and quiet beauty. English writer Jonathan Keates succumbed. "I can't think of anywhere in Italy where I felt safer, more *coccolato* as the Italians say, more cocooned within the embrace of walls and streets. Spello possesses that . . . quality of the ideal Italian town, in which you can see layer upon layer of historical occupation not quite properly absorbed within the layer of brick and stone."

The towns of which I have written in this book in no way encompass the wealth of villages, cities, and tiny collections of ancient farmhouses and towers sprinkled throughout Tuscany and Umbria. Even in the Maremma in the southern coastal region of Tuscany, where charcoal burners, woodsmen, and shepherds until recently wrested a living from the uncompromising landscape of impenetrable thickets of low scrub and dense bushes, there are now elegant summer resorts and half-hidden villas, compact pyramidal villages, and sites like Capalbio, a lovely medieval hill town facing a deeply wooded hill that is now a reserve for wild boar. Once a year when the herds are thinned out, the normally silent town celebrates by turning its piazze, courtyards, steeply winding stone streets, and tiny walled enclosures into outdoor trattorie and rustic kitchens in which great cauldrons of soup are simmered and boar meat is stewed or grilled.

Of course there have been changes since I first wrote of these places. Visitors and citizens arrive at the center of the vibrant city of Perugia through a newly constructed escalator that pierces the remains of the dark underground city, which the ruling Baglioni family built to protect themselves from an enraged citizenry in the sixteenth century. Now people reach the main piazza by traversing the viscera of the medieval past, riding slowly through the mysterious heart of the city, over which rises the Rocca Paolina, the huge fortress built by the pope when he ordered the destruction of the hidden city.

Orvieto, set on an outcropping of porous volcanic rock rising more than six hundred feet above the valley, now rests safely on its foundations. A massive reconstruction project has stabilized and restored the rock, drawing water from its interior and strengthening it with a complicated system of steel bars.

Todi now has a handsome gallery of modern art, and Cortona, described twenty-five years ago in a guide book as a place so silent that "the drumbeats of history could be heard," now hosts students at the art center of an American university as well as a large community of expatriate writers. The artist Niki di San Phalle has created a remarkable fantasy world of sculptures in her Tarot Garden on the outskirts of Pescia Fiorentina, near Capalbio.

In all parts of Tuscany and Umbria, villas and farmhouses, palazzi and convents have been restored as hotels and handsome restaurants for the ever-increasing number of visitors lured by the beauty and timelessness of the heart of Italy. Houses, cottages, *case coloniche*, and villas are offered for rent to vacationers who want to immerse themselves in the peace and harmony of these welcoming landscapes. Farmhouses have become part of the phenomenon called *agritourismo*, whereby travelers stay on working farms, experiencing the hospitality of the countryside; wineries and olive oil estates increasingly attract visitors throughout the year.

Some sights are part of a vanishing tradition. It has become extremely rare to see white oxen or haystacks shaped like houses. Olives planted after the frost of 1985 are likely to be planted as high bushes rather than tall trees simply for the ease of picking. Still, the heart-stopping beauty of this part of Italy and the romance that Richard Kauffman's photographs capture so eloquently continue to lure us to the incomparable regions of Tuscany and Umbria.

These towns grew organically out of their landscapes and out of the stone of the countryside, and they will continue to draw us up their winding roads through thick stone ramparts and narrow medieval gates into a piazza with Romanesque church and Renaissance well, with dark rises of streets that fall steeply away. We will continue to be stirred by slender towers and crenellated battlements, by long rows of vines marching over the fields, by houses with geometry as pure as a Morandi, light and shadow falling across rectangle, square, and recessed cube. Arched doorways, stone carvings, arcaded loggias, vaulted passageways, houses painted with a wash of color: we respond to the economy and simplicity of the materials to stone and brick and muted red tiles and to the seemingly endless variations on their peaceful composition. We are moved by them in wordless ways and so we will continue to return to these towns, for they call to us with their beauty and they reassure us with their permanence.

CAROL FIELD, 1996

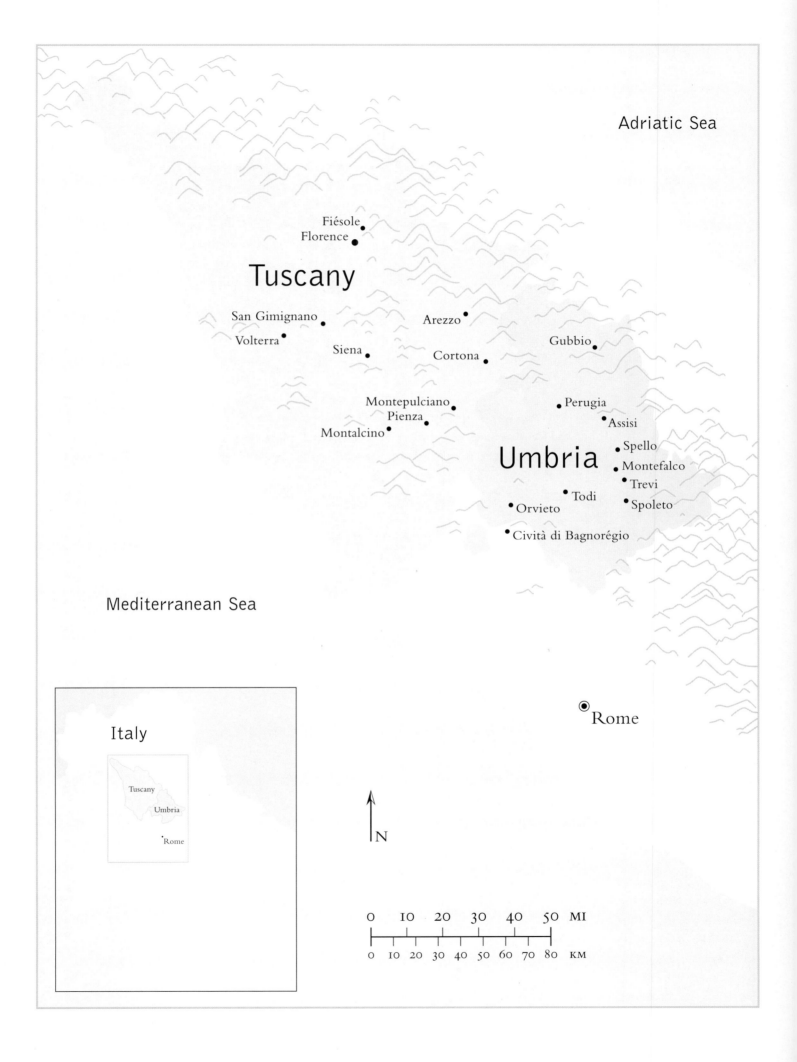

Adriatic Sea

Fiésole
Florence

Tuscany

San Gimignano
Volterra
Siena

Arezzo
Cortona

Gubbio

Perugia
Assisi

Montepulciano
Pienza
Montalcino

Umbria

Spello
Montefalco
Trevi

Todi
Orvieto
Spoleto

Città di Bagnorégio

Mediterranean Sea

Rome

Italy

Tuscany

Umbria

Rome

N

0   10   20   30   40   50   MI

0   10 20 30 40 50 60 70 80   KM

A Short History

An old Italian saying calls Florence the daughter and Rome the mother. What, then, of the hill towns that are older than either, and so predate the larger cities as to make them parvenus? Clinging to the tops of hills like so many Noah's arks after the flood waters receded, they sit isolated and self-contained, the aristocratic outposts of an ancient culture.

Though there are many hill towns throughout Italy, the ones in Tuscany and Umbria are concentrated in the heart of the country and are intimately tied to the long history of Italian civilization. "It is indeed a striking thought," the French expert Jacques Heurgon has written, "that the same region of Italy has twice, in the shape of ancient Etruria and modern Tuscany, been the source of civilization in Italy." These remote sites provided natural defenses for the earliest settlers; later, medieval inhabitants added massive gates, clumps of towers, and a rich variety of architecture. From a distance, these cities, with their walled ramparts, stone fortresses, and cinnamon-colored roofs spilling down steeply canted streets, may have similarities. But each has a profile and personality of its own, its own color and texture from the local stone, and a different configuration of building and public spaces inside. Most have

a *Duomo* (cathedral), *Palazzo Pubblico* or *Communale* (town hall) and *Palazzo Vescovile* (Bishop's Palace), perhaps a *Palazzo del Podestà* or *Palazzo del Capitano del Populo* (Governor's Palace) set around an open piazza where the city celebrates its public festivities. In some, there is a large and conspicuous well, handsomely ornamented to celebrate the importation of water to such heights. Larger cities have two adjoining piazze, and in some, the town hall has a higher tower than the church—evidence of the rivalry between pope and emperor that led to open warfare during the thirteenth and fourteenth centuries.

Despite their medieval appearance, the hill towns of Tuscany and Umbria bear witness to traces of a Bronze Age culture some five millennia old. Whether the original inhabitants were Indo-European invaders who came across the Alps from the north, or traveled by sea across the Adriatic, or were people of an indigenous Apennine culture who moved up the peninsula from the south is still unknown. While historians continue to search for answers, they agree that by about the ninth century B.C., Iron Age horsemen and farmers, known as Villanovans, had penetrated inland to the river valleys of Etruria where they settled upon cliff-like sites. By the

1

eighth century B.C., the Villanovans, who cremated their dead and buried them in urns, had given way to the Etruscans, who transformed their original, naturally fortified settlements into the first cities of central Italy.

The Umbrians, primarily shepherds and warriors, had meanwhile taken possession of a vast region from the Po Valley south to the center of Italy where they, too, grouped their settlements on hilltops and mountain spurs (even today, some fragments remain of the huge walls, built of polygonal stones, which encircled the towns). It wasn't long before the Etruscans challenged the Umbrian inhabitants, forcing them eastward across the Tiber, the most notable natural boundary of the region. Until the Romans began to conquer and colonize the hill towns in the third century B.C., the towns west of the Tiber—such as Perugia and Orvieto—were Etruscan, and those to the east—notably Assisi, Gubbio, and Spoleto—were Umbrian. What little evidence we have of the early Umbrians comes from the bronze Iguvine (or Eugubine) Tablets found at Gubbio many centuries after they were inscribed. Of the seven, engraved between the third and first centuries B.C., five are written in Etruscan letters and two in Latin letters that form Umbrian words describing religious rituals and a priestly code by which they lived. From them it is clear that close similarities linked the religions of Umbria and Etruria, indicating connections between the peoples of the peninsula and a strong Etruscan influence. Yet it appears that the Umbrians, a comparatively rustic, insular, and suspicious people, accepted an alliance with the culturally more advanced and urbane Etruscans only when confronted with the imminent danger presented by the growing power of Rome. By then, however, it was too late and both cultures were eventually conquered and absorbed into the Roman Empire. The distrust with which they initially regarded each other was a pattern that would repeat itself again and again, creating rivalries between hill towns that remain even today.

Before the rise of the Romans, the Etruscans ruled over an enormous area of Italy that included Etruria proper, that portion of the country bounded by the Tyrrhenian Sea and the Arno and Tiber rivers. At the height of their power they controlled fifteen thousand square miles stretching from the Po Valley to the Bay of Naples. As important as Etruscan political rule was, their commercial and cultural influences were far greater. While other peoples of Italy were still living in primitive village cultures, the Etruscans had established a strong urban tradition. Their coastal cities reached greatest importance in the seventh and sixth centuries B.C. The inland cities, most of which were built on rivers, grew later; Orvieto and Chiusi flourished in the fifth century, while Perugia, Arezzo, and Volterra came to greatness in the fourth to second centuries B.C. when Etruscan civilization was already in decline.

Scholars still disagree over the geographical origins of the Etruscans. According to Herodotus, writing in the fifth century B.C., the Etruscans were Lydians who originated in Asia Minor—Vergil even spoke of them interchangeably—but Dionysius of Hallicarnassus, in the century before Christ, contended they were an indigenous tribe grown more sophisticated than their ancestors. Herodotus's theory is buttressed by numerous Etruscan art motifs similar to Near Eastern styles, by the resemblances between Etruscan and Lydian tombs, and by the Etruscan practice of soothsaying, which recalls the ancient Babylonian practice in Asia Minor. Dionysius argued persuasively that the Etruscans had a different religion and spoke a different language than the Lydians, and since no evidence exists of a massive sea migration between 1300 and 700 B.C., when vast changes occurred in the development of this civilization, uncertainties remain to this day.

The puzzle is deepened by the mystery of the Etruscan language, which, unlike most tongues of Europe, is not an Indo-European language. Even though its alphabet derives from the Greek, and extant words can be read and pronounced by experts, no parallel text exists to function as a Rosetta stone in decoding the language. All that remains of original sources are fragmentary funerary and votive inscriptions, for all the literature has been lost, and with it the most lively and vital aspects of the language.

We do know that the Etruscans called themselves Rasenna, although the Greeks knew them as Tyrrhenoi, which name has been given to the sea bordering their lands, and the Romans wrote of them as Etrusci or Tusci, from which the name Tuscany derives. They transformed the villages of the Villanovans into the first real cities of Italy and became a culture of mariners, metalworkers, traders, and artisans. "Etruria filled the whole length of Italy with her name," the Roman historian Livy wrote. Their civilization flourished and Etruscans dominated Rome, where their kings ruled from 616 to 510 B.C. There they drained the marshy valley of what later became the Forum in Rome with sewers that predate the great Cloaca Maxima, paving the reclaimed ground and making it the center of the city. From the Etruscans the Romans learned also the use of the arch and the vault and the art and science of constructing bridges.

In the mountains of Tuscany the Etruscans mined iron, tin, and copper, using charcoal from the forests to power smelting refineries. Trade with the Greeks and their colonies in Sicily and Ionia brought them into contact with Greek art, whose influence may be seen in the crafts that grew up in Etruscan cities: pottery, gold work, and above all bronze transformed into household objects, mirrors, tools, chandeliers, weapons, and works of sculpture like the *Chimera* of Arezzo and the *Mars* of Todi. Their passion for Greek art was so great that it is said that the tombs of Etruria have yielded more Greek vases than Greece itself.

Religion shaped the entire Etruscan civilization. Each town was essentially a theocracy, ruled by a priest-king called a *lucumon*, and it was considered a small fraction of the universal order. The twelve major cities were physically isolated and politically independent, but once a year each sent delegates to a religious meeting at a famous shrine of the goddess Voltumna, near Volsinii, which was considered the heart of the nation.

The Etruscans were the first inhabitants to cultivate the heavily forested region and give it the agrarian character it has had for centuries. The land that they found was shaped by the backbone of the powerful Apennine Mountains, which arc around Tuscany and stretch the entire length of Umbria. In their sweep they change from the massive limestone Apuan Alps with the famous marble of Carrara to the sandstone shales and clays of the upper Arno and Umbrian Apennines to the interior massifs and steep narrow valleys that give way to the wide basins of the Val Tiberina and Val di Chiana. Then, two to five million years ago, during the Pliocene epoch, the basins between the wooded mountains in the interior were invaded by the Tyrrhenian Sea, and the inundations of water eroded the mountains and created the endless hilly undulations where people later chose to locate their hilltop towns. The waters left deposits of limestone and sands in the folds and valleys of the landscape, making the fertile soils where vines and olives and grains grow today. Most of Tuscany between the Arno and Ombrone is hill and plateau, while the area from Monte Amiata to the south and east was formed by volcanic eruptions that were first marked in the Colline Metallifere, the "metal-bearing hills," near the Tuscan coast. For the early Etruscan settlers, the volcanic countryside had much to offer: soft, easily worked soils of great fertility; high,

defensible sites; and, in the west, minerals that gave Etruria great importance in the ancient world.

The fertility of the land, especially the "opulent fields of Etruria" in the region of the upper Tiber, was described enthusiastically by ancient writers. "In a fat soil, as in Etruria," wrote Varro in the first century B.C., "one sees fertile fields that are never fallow, fine straight trees, and no moss anywhere." The Etruscan granaries supplied Rome with grain and were instrumental in providing Scipio Africanus with enough provisions to enable him to sail against Carthage. To make use of the potential fertility of much of the land, the Etruscans had first to drain marshes and harness water for irrigating arid land. Where erosion and flooding were problems, the Etruscans created a complicated series of underground tunnels that drew off the accumulated water and channeled it to nearby rivers or streams, and thereby made hundreds of previously uncultivated acres available for farming. Some of the tunnels, called *cuniculi* by the Romans, are still visible at Chiusi.

The harvests that followed were so rich that the Etruscans were able to export cereal grains, wine from grapes grown in Chianti and the areas around Arezzo, and the pecorino cheese that is still made from sheep's milk in Tuscany today. In addition, the land supported herds of pigs—which fed on acorns from the oak forests that covered the higher slopes—along with cattle and poultry. The forests and marshes were full of birds and abundant game—boar, deer, and hare—and the lakes were well stocked with fish. Etruscan husbandry anticipated the mixed agriculture that can be seen in some places in the region today, with vines supported by trees stretching above plots of grain, filtering the sunlight and screening the crops from the wind. Although the hills of Tuscany and Umbria are filled with olive trees, they appear not to have been planted until after Etruscan times, since olive oil was imported from Greece in the clay amphorae that have been found in numerous tombs.

The early Umbrians and Etruscans chose to build their cities on the heights, not only for the healthy air and for their setting above the lake beds that remained in some places, but also to leave the minimal agricultural flatland free for cultivation. They knew as well that from their lofty vantage points they could safely track the approach of any invaders. Centuries later, when Goths, Vandals, and Lombards invaded the country, the remaining population stayed behind the city walls on the hilltops, clinging to them for protection, and the medieval city-states grew on these same sites almost a millennium later, as if coming to life after a long dark sleep.

When the Romans came to Etruria they found cultivated fields set between forests. They planted wheat and barley, millet and rye, introduced the olive, continued planting vines and making wine, and greatly expanded the numbers and kinds of crops. Small farms gave way to larger landholdings. In the empire, when cheap grain was imported from abroad, oil and wine exports declined, and a great number of acres were transformed for the rearing of livestock. Internal crises and wars shaped the policy of resettling veterans on land confiscated from farmers, often with noticeably poor results. With the mounting economic crisis and rapid decline of the empire, the Roman drainage system fell into decay, cattle grazed once-fertile fields, and extensive areas returned to swamp. The Val di Chiana reverted to marsh, and the Maremma became a notorious pestilential haunt, fit only for snakes in Dante's day and for sheep in their winter pasturage into this century.

The legendary fertility of Tuscany and Umbria varies within the regions. The Val di Chiana, with its intense mixed cultivation, is now one of the richest agricultural areas of Tuscany since eighteenth- and nineteenth-century engineers channeled the waters of the Chiani River into the Arno, as the Romans had once planned, and drained the perpetually marshy valley floor. Aggressive reform in this century has rehabilitated the Maremma and made it significantly more productive. Of the dense forests that once covered the land before the Etruscans and Romans exploited them for timber and cleared the land for agricultural use, a mere fraction still stands. Although farmers have continually pushed far up the hillsides with their crops, the richness and fertility of the soils make this among the most desirable and carefully planted land on the Italian peninsula.

The Etruscans had two centuries of greatness, but in 510 B.C. a well-planned revolt by the Romans broke the succession of Etruscan kings. Livy says that the Roman Senate trembled when the great Etruscan king Lars Porsena rode to Rome to demand the return to the throne of Tarquinius, his deposed countryman, and while some sources say his campaign was successful, most record the attempt a failure. The Etruscans were defeated decisively at the battle of Aricia four years later and the Roman Republic was preserved. With the defeat of Etruscan sea power by the Sicilian Greeks in 474 B.C. and the arrival shortly thereafter of the Gauls from the north who pushed them inland, the belea-

guered Etruscans became less and less able to defend themselves, and by the end of the third century B.C., they had submitted totally to Roman authority and cast their lot with the republic.

All that is now left to us of Etruria is collected in museums, for although the cemeteries and tombs of its people are everywhere—buried in ravines or deep in tufa gorges, hidden beneath the dark green tangles of underbrush on wooded cliffs—they are largely empty, having been rifled by the tomb robbers of the past. Necropolises and tombs like the vaulted meloni at Cortona, the great tumulus at Castellina in Chianti, or the famous tombs at the foot of the hills of Perugia, Orvieto, and Chiusi can be seen dotting the landscape, but the Etruscans simply disappeared as they became overshadowed by the grandeur of Rome. As a result, Tuscany's first civilization was eclipsed until the Etruscomania of the eighteenth century won some recognition for the ancestral figures who gave life to these hilltops and brought fertility to its valleys. The architect and painter Giambattista Piranesi, who went to Cortona to copy friezes from the walls of its Etruscan tombs, became passionately convinced that the art of ancient Italy was indigenous and not the product of learning from the Greeks. It was he who discovered, in reconstructing the Rome of the Tarquin kings, that in fact the Roman arch and the vault were invented by the Etruscans.

In the city-states that rose after the Etruscan decline, the same imaginative and artistic vitality seemed to breathe again after the long dark winter of the barbarian invasions. "For who knows, even today," wrote Osbert Sitwell in *Great Morning!*, "the ancestry of that mysterious race, or whence came the originals of those enigmatic effigies that can still be seen reclining upon their funerary urns in rock sepulcher and museum; figures with slanting eyebrows and brooding, incalculable smiles; characteristics to be repeated, over and over again, many hundreds of years later, in the Florentine pictures, and to be observed to this day, exemplified in the eager, rustic faces of the Tuscan peasants."

Unlike Etruria, which has vanished, the Roman civilization that absorbed it is visible in architectural fragments, especially amphitheaters, baths, and temples, and in the mathematically precise city plan that can still be discerned beneath the medieval structure of some hill towns. But it is the network of roads that is the principal memorial of the domination of Rome. The Via Aurelia followed the curve of Tuscany's western shore and was

Floor detail, Duomo, Spoleto

5

later extended to Pisa and Lucca; the Via Flaminia ran through the Umbrian heart of the peninsula to the northern frontier and the Adriatic; and the Via Cassia was the main road between Rome and Florence, passing through Chiusi and Arezzo before eventually joining Bologna. Like the major highways, smaller roads ran north and south in Tuscany and Umbria. The Via Clodia cut across the western edge of Tuscany, the Via Amerina reached into southern Umbria, and the Via Tiberina followed the Tiber Valley parallel to the Via Flaminia before crossing the river at Ocriculum.

When Rome conquered territories, she treated cities differently. Some were made allies, some given limited Roman citizenship, and some created as new military colonies and peopled with Romans. All roads literally led to Rome because the consular highways played a primary role in control and communication within the country. Unlike the Etruscans, who constructed a network of roads by following the contours of geography, the Romans disregarded obstacles and drove straight to their destination, using bridges or paved fords to cross rivers and massive viaducts to traverse marshy land.

All the hill towns originally fought against the Romans. By the beginning of the third century B.C., however, the Etruscan cities of Arezzo, Cortona, and Chiusi had been occupied, and though some others had formed an alliance against the Romans, they, too, had been subjugated by the time Hannibal arrived with the first major challenge to the Romans' authority. A brilliant visionary, the Carthaginian Hannibal had been determined since childhood to destroy the Romans for their victory over his city in the First Punic War. In the autumn of 218 B.C., he came over the Alps with an assemblage of mercenaries, Spanish, Ligurian, and Libyan infantry, Numidian horsemen, and Moroccan elephants, and began his march through central Italy. On the shores of Lake Trasimeno, near Perugia, Hannibal devised his strategy for luring Flaminius, the Roman commander, into an ambush where some fifteen thousand Romans died, including Flaminius himself, and another fifteen thousand were taken prisoner. Proceeding across the Tiber to the walls of Spoleto, Hannibal expected to be welcomed with enthusiasm by the citizens, as a liberator from the Romans. Instead, they rose against him, driving him back at a spot that is known today as the Porta Fuga, or the Gate of Flight. And although a number of city-states in southern Italy did become his allies, Hannibal's effort at conquest eventually failed.

Rome was the first power to unify the entire Italian peninsula. Some of the hill towns played major roles under its rule, while others, such as Siena, Orvieto, and Cortona, have few buildings or ruins from that time. Todi was a military camp; Gubbio, a religious center and strategic site guarding the Via Flaminia in its isolated post between Rome and Ravenna. Perugia, which had suffered for putting up the fiercest fight against Roman domination and was half destroyed during the civil war between Mark Antony and Octavian, was originally a regional center. Spoleto boasted more Roman buildings and monuments than any other Umbrian hill town, as a sign of Rome's gratitude for repelling Hannibal. Spello was an important imperial center and Arezzo a prosperous city on the Via Cassia, producing red glazed pottery that was widely exported throughout the ancient world.

But as Rome's supremacy expanded abroad, there were political crises at home and the republic was undermined by civil wars. In the year 91 B.C., disaffected Italians, including some Etruscans and Umbrians, joined the Samnites in an uprising known as the Social War, and as a political concession to all who rebelled and surrendered, the Romans granted citizenship under the Julian Law. A second uprising was put down by the general Sulla, with mass executions of those who defied him. The Etruscans were singled out for punishment because of their determined resistance, and they suffered such devastation that they never recovered. Land was confiscated from Volterra, Arezzo, and Chiusi in Etruria and from Todi and Spoleto in Umbria. Half a century later, unhappy soldiers who had been forced to settle in Tuscany as a result of the Sullan wars rebelled at the urging of Catiline, whose conspiracy Cicero exposed. The assassination of Julius Caesar ended his effort to bring peace to the region, which under Augustus was administered as Region VII, "in which is Etruria," and Region VI, which appeared for the first time as "Umbria."

Octavian—who became Augustus in 27 B.C.—ruled for the forty-five years that were the most creative period of Roman civilization. He reformed almost every institution, presided over an era of intensive building, and established the empire on such firm footing that it endured for four centuries more. And he created a durable Roman peace that made possible the transmission of the Greco-Roman heritage.

The empire, reaching from the Black Sea to the Atlantic, and from Britain to the deserts of Africa, had grown too large to be ruled by a single leader. While slaves and mercenaries fueled the economy, the land was neglected as farmers were conscripted into the army and small holdings were absorbed by enormous estates. During the reign of Marcus Aurelius (emperor A.D. 161–80), hordes of Germans first crossed the Alps, attacking Roman territories. Although these forays were settled when some of the barbarians were permitted to remain, in time the Romans were confronted with new invaders in the Goths, who migrated south and surged across the Danube. Shortly after, the eastern frontier was threatened by still other Germanic tribes. To protect the country, the imperial army was compelled to divide itself into an eastern and western command, anticipating the later division of the empire.

During the third century A.D., the emperor Diocletian reorganized the government by partitioning the empire into four areas, each with its own ruler and capital. He reformed the administration of government and annexed Umbria to Tuscany, calling the entire area Tuscia, although the strip along the Tiber and a portion of its southern territory were sliced away in the tenth century when all of central Italy was divided between the Lombard and Byzantine empires. Under Constantine the Great (emperor A.D. 306–37), the empire acquired a new eastern capital in Constantinople, a new army, and an official religion in Christianity. In 364 the emperor Valentinian I officially divided the empire into Western and Eastern parts; while he ruled from Milan, his brother was in Constantinople and the now powerless Senate remained in Rome.

During the reign of these two emperors, two major events set the stage for the swift disintegration of the empire. Savage Mongol hordes, under their leader Attila the Hun, appeared in about 370, and even the Goths were unable to withstand their assaults. A large number of them, both Visigoths and Ostrogoths, crossed into the empire, and in 378 a Gothic army defeated the Roman army of the East and the emperor Valens was slain. From the death of his successor, Theodosius—who held the empire together for a time—to the collapse of the Western Empire was only a matter of time, as waves of barbarian invaders confronted the army and devastated city after city. The Visigoth leader Alaric occupied Rome, while the king of the Vandals invaded North Africa. In 476, Odoacer, a barbarian chief, exposed the fiction of the Western Empire in deposing its last emperor and crowning himself king.

Even before the Western Empire succumbed, monks and bishops in mountaintop communities and remote hermitages were quietly filling the vacuum left by the breakdown of order and were becoming the civil and spiritual leaders of Umbria. There were twenty-two bishops in as many cities, but the most important figure of the time was Benedict, who founded the great Benedictine monastery of Monte Cassino.

Benedict was born in the remote eastern area of Nursia in about 480, just as the empire was crumbling, and his life was shaped by early years spent as a hermit in a cave on Monte Subiaco where he endured "the solitary combat of the desert" and where he began to formulate a vision developed after years of contemplation. He did not enunciate the Benedictine Rule until near the end of his life, but he had long lived by the categorical imperative of *Ora et labora* (Pray and work), and it was his sense of contributing to the material well-being of society while working in spiritual solitude that distinguished the Benedictine tradition. He inspired men to follow him in serving the world in practical ways, and countless of them, following his leadership, cultivated the earth and made it fertile again, preserved and copied manuscripts of antiquity, and kept alive a respect for learning during the worst of the Dark Ages.

The isolation and remoteness of Umbria attracted seekers after solitude and reflection. The Franciscan and Benedictine monasteries that were subsequently established all over Europe have their roots in Umbrian soil where Christianity was nourished from its infancy. Religion provided consolation and gave form to the suffering inflicted on the people, as the country endured the ravages of plague and the devastation of barbarian invaders and vicious emperors.

After Totila, the brilliant leader of the Goths, became master of southern and central Italy, the Eastern emperor Justinian sent an army under his great general Belisarius to destroy Totila and his forces, restore the empire, and recapture Rome. The region was a battleground for twenty years, and in the roll call of cities devastated by Totila and the armies that opposed him were Fiesole and Chiusi in Tuscany, Perugia, Assisi, Orvieto, and Gubbio, along with Spoleto and Spello. Of the Umbrian towns, only Todi, under its aptly named Bishop Fortunato, managed to escape the Gothic forces that ranged across the landscape, burning and killing, terrorizing the population before Totila was finally trapped and killed high in the mountain town of Gualdo Tadino.

Before the cities of Tuscany and Umbria could begin to recover, the incursion of the Germanic

Lombards began. These "back woodsmen who had swooped down upon the land of Vergil," as described by Janet Trevelyan in *A Short History of the Italian People*, ruled Tuscany from their local capital at Lucca, and Umbria from ducal headquarters in Spoleto, for 250 years, dominating most of the peninsula until 774. By then they had renounced their barbarism, adopted the language of their Italian subjects, and converted to their religion, building great abbeys alongside their castles. The desire of the Lombard rulers to add the dukedom of Spoleto, which encompassed much of central Italy, to the territory of their northern kingdom, with its capital at Pavia, and their southern duchy of Benevento, was frustrated when the Popes allied themselves with the Franks, yet another Germanic tribe. In the year 800, after the Frankish king Charlemagne had incorporated the Lombard monarchy into his own domain, Pope Leo III crowned him Emperor at Rome. With that stroke he created a Western Empire that split the peninsula into two parts, one imperial and one papal, which would not be united again until the nineteenth century. As Latin Christianity shifted its center from Byzantium (Constantinople) to Rome, the Papal States—an amalgam of the geographical splinters of central Italy that included Byzantine and Lombard holdings—became an aggressive power. They based their legitimacy on a bold and clever forgery known as the Donation of Constantine, which claimed that the first Christian emperor had transferred the rule of central Italy to the Popes. Charlemagne's authentication of the forgery essentially validated the political supremacy of the Popes over Rome, Italy, and the whole Western world and justified their interference in the affairs of Umbrian cities. Thus the stage was set for a conflict that would endure for five hundred years.

Charlemagne's successors, as rulers of the Holy Roman Empire, tried to control their territory in Italy, with varying degrees of success. While the Emperors sought to unite Italy under their control, the Popes were equally determined to free the Church from imperial control and maintain their own power. The early Middle Ages saw the enmity ripen into an intense rivalry whose violent passions were characteristic of the times.

In Tuscany the flame was lit as the Lombard duchy with its local capital at Lucca became a Frankish margravate, which passed into the hands of Matilda, Countess of Tuscany, whose inherited family lands covered much of northern Italy. She was a friend of Pope Gregory VII, the first great papal reformer. Gregory assumed office in 1073 with strong ideas of making the Church the supreme power in the Christian world. Almost immediately he set about purging the Church of married clergy and prohibiting the secular appointment of bishops and abbots—a change of policy that was a direct challenge to rulers who counted on the revenues they obtained from the sale of such offices, and who depended on the allegiance of the bishops who had lands and armies of their own.

When Henry IV of Germany, King and Holy Roman Emperor, making it clear that he didn't plan to give up his rights, proceeded to name his own German bishops, Gregory sent a messenger commanding the Emperor to appear in Rome and explain his actions. Henry refused, and the Pope promptly excommunicated him. Realizing that he would have to submit to the Pope to keep his title, Henry decided to meet him, since he was traveling north, at Matilda's castle at Canossa. Aware that he held the upper hand, the Pope retreated inside and kept the Emperor waiting at the castle gates for three long winter days. Even Matilda, as a good Catholic, was shocked at such treatment of the secular head of Christendom.

Gregory granted Henry absolution, but that was not the end of their warfare. The Pope excommunicated Henry again, and the King took his revenge by twice besieging Rome. He was unsuccessful the first time, but on the second, when he could find no one to crown him Emperor—all his bishops having been excommunicated—he created a second Pope and proceeded to ravage Rome with such ferocity that Gregory was forced into exile, where he died.

This conflict lit a deadly spark in the historic warfare of Popes and Emperors that split Italy and kept it a country divided for centuries. The division traced its roots to differences deep in the blood. The nobles, who had conquered the country in the dark centuries after the fall of the empire, were mostly Germanic—Lombards, Franks, and Carolingians—while the old Romans, who had remained in the crumbling cities during the barbarian invasions, were Latin, and this antagonism, between feudal lord and urban dweller, Teuton and Latin, was expressed in savage battles until the cities made war upon the unregenerate nobles and forced them within the compass of their walls.

The cities began to rebuild their defenses to guard against the encroachments of rival nobles who had first brought factionalism to the countryside as they swooped down from their hilltop castles and pounced on travelers, demanding a kind of ransom for the privilege of continuing their journeys. With brute force

Stained glass window and candelabra, Duomo, Perugia

Franciscan monks, Assisi

the nobles plundered and devastated the area, and the countryside was soon covered with the castles of feudal lords who made life almost impossible for the people inadvertently trapped in their feuds and vendettas. In self-defense the people fled and, like filings attracted by a powerful magnet, collected within city walls. In time the cities grew stronger, augmenting their defenses, expanding their authority, and extending their frontiers by buying or conquering castles in the countryside.

At first each city had at least one castle, the urbanized equivalent of the watchtower of the country, but as time passed, almost every town became a virtual forest bristling with these constructions of cobbles and lime that stood ready to enclose a whole retinue of warriors and extended family when private disputes erupted into open warfare. Competition between rival families or between branches of the same family often dictated

the heights of the towers, which were inspired as much by social status and desire for upward mobility as they were by fear and military necessity. And when danger of external invasion passed, the aggressive instincts of the city dwellers turned inward and the slender shafts of stone stood like giant sundials, casting shadows that warned of the impending violence that would erupt within the walls.

A century after Gregory made his challenge to the emperor, the struggle was renewed. Frederick Hohenstaufen, whom the Italians called Barbarossa or Red Beard—whether for its natural color or for the blood that stained it, at least figuratively, is not clear— arrived in Italy, intending to reassert the claims of the empire. Following his coronation in 1155, when even Rome refused to receive him, he arrived in Spoleto and demanded tribute as the city's imperial overlord. When he did not receive it, he personally led an attack that lasted for six hours. And when it was over, the Germans were in charge, looting and burning, destroying the cathedral, and routing the citizens, who took refuge on the slopes of Monte Luco. By the time Barbarossa died in 1190, he had little to show for his invasions and had in fact been forced to confirm the independence of the very cities he had meant to subjugate. His defeat was a historic victory for the communes of central Italy, which counted the beginnings of their autonomy from that moment.

As the fortunes of the empire declined, the region saw the ascendancy of Pope Innocent III, whose strategy was to form a political alliance of Umbrian cities. He wooed Assisi away from imperial control, forming a Guelph league supporting the papal party along with Todi, Perugia, and Spoleto. And he formed a more unlikely alliance with the barefoot, shabbily robed followers of a young man from Assisi who was to become St. Francis. As a practical man of the world, the Pope had been inclined to dismiss Francis and the rigorous poverty he practiced until the night when he had a dream of seeing the Church of San Giovanni in Laterano about to fall, only to be saved by the small figure in rustic clothes who had come to see him that day. Believing the dream was a portent, Innocent called Francis back and—at a time when many were repelled by the worldliness and corruption of the Church— gave provisional permission for the formation of the Franciscan order.

Like the early disciples of Jesus, Francis and his followers lived with extreme simplicity, preaching and sharing the work of the people of the countryside. As he walked through Umbria, Francis captured the hearts of the people and left a legend wherever he went: of taming a wolf at Gubbio; of preaching to the birds at Bevagna; and of so inspiring the people at Cannara that every single one of them wanted to follow him. His simple delight in the beauty of the natural world and his joyful identification with every living creature were like the rays of a warm sun after the chilly monasticism of the early Middle Ages. The Franciscans radically transformed the religious life of Italy and were a harbinger of the artistic awakening that would ripen into the Renaissance. Francis had a profound influence on Giotto, whose visual language was based on observations from nature, and on Dante, who wrote in Italian rather than Latin and created a picture of life based on the world around him.

As St. Francis embodied the religious aspect of the Middle Ages, Frederick II exemplified its secular concerns. The only one of the so-called Holy Roman Emperors to grow up in Italy, Frederick was a grandson of Barbarossa and as a Hohenstaufen he had inherited the Norman kingdom of Naples and Sicily. Called Stupor Mundi (Wonder of the World) by his admirers, he considered himself destined to reconquer Rome and make it the center of the empire once again. When Pope Honorius III crowned Frederick Emperor in 1220 and three years later gave final approval to the Franciscan movement, he set the stage for the conflict between Pope and Emperor in which both sides were essentially defeated. And from that defeat rose a secularized society whose advent marked the end of the Middle Ages.

During this time, Tuscany and Umbria were a collection of communes, a patchwork whose boundaries shifted without warning as cities began to feel their strength and pounce upon neighboring territory. From year to year, according to Geoffrey Trease in *The Italian Story*, the map resembled "some animated biological diagram, depicting cells in a feverish alternation of union and fission." Changing loyalties make it difficult to keep straight the alliances of any one city, much less its internal rivalries and schisms, but the basic division was between the Guelphs, who took the part of the Pope and budding capitalists, and the Ghibellines, who represented the Holy Roman Emperor and the feudal nobility. Their names entered the political vocabulary of Italy during the reign of Frederick II, when the latter were named for the Hohenstaufen castle of Wibeling and the former for the Welf Saxons whom the Popes had supported. The dominant party determined a town's allegiance, and a quick glance at the shape of a town's battlements told the tale: those of the Guelphs were square at the top while those of the Ghibellines were forked, or swallow-tailed. Allegiances were determined as much by expedience as by tradition, and in fact the towns manipulated the alliances for their own ends. Even within towns there were schisms within Guelph and Ghibelline factions, and the party out of power was always in exile, plotting vicious schemes of revenge.

Every hill town extended its power over the countryside until it bumped into the territory of a neighboring town, which was inevitably its most powerful enemy. The nearer the towns, the more virulent the rivalry, so that Perugia and Assisi, located a mere fifteen miles apart, were often at war, as were Florence and Siena, each wanting to dominate Tuscany. Florence, banker to the Papacy, was Guelph; so Siena, also a banking and mercantile city, was naturally Ghibelline. Throughout Tuscany, as Mary McCarthy points out in *The Stones of Florence*, the politics, like the architecture, tended to be black and white; if the allegiance of one town changed, so in turn did the next, always keeping the basic black-and-white pattern, and the smaller cities were always at the mercy of the larger ones that wanted to dominate the area. Many times a fresh military defeat was all it took to rearrange the political checkerboard with new allies and allegiances.

The struggle for supremacy in Umbria took place on several fronts. The Popes who had established control of the region shrewdly used the power of the Franciscans and other mendicants for their own ends, while Frederick II tried numerous schemes for enlisting local enthusiasms in the cause of the Ghibellines. Time and again he was confronted by the Franciscan tertiaries, an order of laymen who were active in society as an expression of their religious conviction. The members of the order challenged the basic assumptions of feudalism when they refused to fight and instead pledged themselves to a spirit of cooperation. As they grew in numbers their influence also grew, and Frederick ultimately blamed them for frustrating his own efforts. By 1244 every major Umbrian city had resisted the designs of empire and had again become allied with the Guelphs, the party of the papacy. After Frederick II died in 1250, his illegitimate son Manfred made an effort of his own to become master of Italy. His strategy led to a radical shift of power in Tuscany when Florence was defeated by Siena in the battle of Montaperti, in the year 1260; altogether, ten thousand of her men were killed and fifteen thousand others were captured by the Ghibelline forces. Terrified that Manfred would destroy the power of the papacy, Pope Urban IV, a Frenchman who took office determined to be rid of "this brood of vipers," as he called the Hohenstaufens, ordered Christians to default on their debts to the Sienese banks that had financed Manfred. Then he offered the crown of Naples and Sicily to Charles of Anjou, brother of the French king. Charles proceeded to raise an army of thirty thousand, and in 1266 Manfred was defeated and slain in the battle of Benevento. Within four years Charles had reversed the situation and became master of Tuscany, where he ruled for three years more. Even his allies found him unlovable—while Manfred, a poet as well as a knight— had been appealing even to his enemies in spite of his

Fields, hedges, and cypresses were tipped with an aureate brightness which recalled the golden ripples running over the grass in the foreground of Botticelli's "Birth of Venus." The sunshine had the density of gold-leaf; we seemed to be driving through the landscape of a missal.

EDITH WHARTON
Italian Backgrounds

success against the Ghibellines. The papacy, which had injected a foreign power into Italian politics, would live to regret the situation, first when it moved to Avignon for most of the fourteenth century, and again in 1494 when the French king rode over the Apennines with an invading army.

Following the death of Manfred, the cities of Tuscany and Umbria came into flower as independent communities while the power of both Church and Emperor declined. In 1309 the strength and influence of the Church were greatly diminished when Pope Clement V moved the papal see to Avignon, and the Holy Roman Emperors' ambitions came to nothing after the death of Frederick II. A new bourgeoisie, represented by powerful trade guilds, now became predominant, challenging the authority of the old urban aristocracy. The old Guelph and Ghibelline factions survived, as the Guelphs, once associated with the papacy, came to stand for the newly emergent middle class, while the Ghibellines became the party of the aristocracy. The city-states devised the development of a new form of constitutional government, under the authority of a *podestà*, who was brought in from another town in an effort to achieve impartiality, and a *capitano del populo*, who functioned as the military chief. A clever *capitano* could capitalize on continued political tensions and use his position as a first step toward one-man rule. *Signoria*, rule by a single man or by members of a single family, became increasingly common as communes were confronted with wars in the countryside and internal factions struggling for control. The exterior security provided by well-fortified walls and towers allowed the conflicts of the time to turn inward, where they took the form of suicidal vendettas. At San Gimignano, for example, the feud between the Ardinghelli and the Salvucci so devastated the life of the city that it was finally forced to cede itself to Florence and ask the city to dictate its own terms of acceptance.

The rise of tyranny, with provincial despots making civil decisions, and the prevalence of mercenaries who fought for pay annihilated the republican institutions that had grown up in the towns. *Condottieri*, those enterprising commanders who sold their services to the highest bidder, freed the citizens from having to go to war and left them to amass the wealth that funded the great cultural works that gave splendor to the time. But the price was appallingly high. Money replaced spiritual authority and corrupted the society at every level. What Leonardo Olschki calls, in *The Genius of*

Farmhouse near Orvieto

Italy, the "commercialization of power," which allowed city dwellers to build their extraordinary palaces and churches and freed artisans to consolidate themselves into increasingly powerful guilds, led ultimately to the destruction of their own civil liberties.

The crisis became acute after the Black Death of 1348, which depleted many towns by as much as or more than half their population. The disorder and demoralization that followed opened the way for marauding mercenaries under the control of *condottieri* such as Fortebraccio, Gattamelata, and Piccinino, and for foreign soldiers of fortune such as Sir John Hawkwood. Economic decline brought retreat. At the same time that the Sienese abandoned their grand plans for expanding the Duomo into the greatest cathedral in Italy, an intense spiritual revival grew up around the young mystic Catherine of Siena. It was she, as much as anyone, who would eventually persuade Pope Gregory XI to end the "Babylonian Captivity" and return to Rome. During intervening decades, Pope Innocent VI had set about the rebuilding of papal authority from Avignon, entrusting the task to his legate, the Spanish Cardinal Albornoz. For fourteen years Albornoz ranged throughout Umbria, leveling castle after castle in a massive effort to carry out the dream of a papal state in central Italy. The great fortresses he built at Assisi and Spoleto are monuments to his success, although he had failures elsewhere, notably at Perugia, which rejected his efforts.

In Tuscany, Florence became the chief power and continued to expand its conquests, even though 40 percent of its population had died of the plague in 1348. Pisa, Livorno, Montepulciano, Arezzo, and Cortona came under its domination during the fourteenth century, leaving only Siena and Volterra of the Tuscan hill towns still free of its clutches. The rediscovery of the classical past brought a surge of artistic energy to fifteenth-century Florence, where the concentration of wealth in the hands of individual aristocratic patrons transformed the look of the city.

The greatest of these patrons were the family of the Medici, who came to power in 1421 with Giovanni, the founder of the dynasty. His son the elder Cosimo de'Medici, a consummate financier who multiplied his fortune many times over through his operations as a banker, ruled the city for thirty years, maintaining republican forms as he consolidated his power. He and his son Piero and his grandson Lorenzo after him were statesmen and humanists who all supported the arts with extraordinary generosity, as the patrons of Leon Battista

Alberti, Donatello, Fra Angelico, the Della Robias, and Benozzo Gozzoli, and later of Botticelli, Verrocchio, Ghirlandaio, Michelangelo, Leonardo, and the poet Angelo Poliziano. Lorenzo escaped death at the hands of the Pazzi conspirators, who stabbed and killed his brother while they were receiving the Host at mass; and he eventually won out over Pope Sixtus IV, who had instigated the conspiracy. During the rule of Lorenzo, who was known as *il Magnifico* (the Magnificent), the city was enriched by works of art and by an intellectual brilliance that rivaled the civilization of Periclean Athens. The sixteenth-century historian Guicciardini wrote of him: "In short, we must needs conclude that under him the city was not free, but that it would have been impossible to have found a better or more agreeable tyrant; for his natural goodness of disposition produced innumerable benefits, while the fact of his tyranny caused also certain evils, tempered and limited by the bounds of necessity."

Lorenzo's death in 1492 robbed Italy of its chief statesman and keeper of the peace. It was one of the events of a watershed year that gave the kaleidoscope of history a sharp shake, unsettling the pieces into new patterns and alignments. France for the first time had an energetic king who unified the country. While the Dominican friar Savonarola was predicting an approaching catastrophe in which the sins of a worldly and pagan society would be punished, Charles VIII of France rode into Tuscany with a great army, on his way to claim the throne of Naples. He was met by Piero, the cowardly son of Lorenzo de' Medici, who had fled from Florence in panic but who now threw himself at the feet of the French king, giving him the keys of the fortresses that guarded the Tuscan state. Rumor of this craven surrender preceded his return to Florence, and he was immediately ridden out of the city as a traitor. His legacy to Tuscany was to leave it a battlefield between the French, who occupied Florence in his wake, and the Spanish, who challenged their invasion, and for the next sixty years the two powers carved up the cities and their countryside. Savonarola, who rose to take Piero's place, greeted Charles as the city's deliverer, sure that his wrath would purge Florence of its sins. A mere four years later, Savonarola himself was arrested, tortured, tried, and condemned for heresy, and he was executed in the very piazza that had witnessed the "Burning of Vanities" to which his sermons had incited the people of Florence.

Eighteen years passed between the expulsion of Piero and the return of the Medici to Florence. The

Medici Pope Clement VII allied himself with the French against the Spanish emperor Charles V, who took revenge when his armies sacked Rome in 1527 and the fury of their destruction forced the Pope to hide in the Castel Sant' Angelo. The Florentines saw their advantage, rebelled against the Medici, and then raised an army to resist the restoration of a Medici government. They were prepared three years later when Clement led an assault using the same vicious mercenary soldiers of the Spanish emperor, who was now his ally, but they were undone by the treachery of Malatesta Baglioni, their own commander in chief, who sold the city to her enemies. The Emperor's army, allowed to enter the city, brought the flowering of the Renaissance to an abrupt and bloody halt.

With the final loss of freedom, the rule of the Medicean dukes began. Among Tuscan towns, only Siena and Lucca remained holdouts against their control. In 1554 the armies of Cosimo I, in league with those of the Spanish emperor, began a fifteen-month siege of Siena. Behind the city walls people fell dead in the streets from hunger, and those who ventured out were cut down until, as one observer wrote, "the trees seemed to bear dead men." When the Sienese were finally forced to surrender, the population had fallen from forty thousand to ten thousand. Shortly thereafter the city became part of the Medici holdings, Cosimo I was made Grand Duke of Tuscany in 1569, and his rule of the hill towns of Tuscany was complete.

As the commander Albornoz had done in Umbria, Cosimo I strung a powerful chain of fortresses throughout the hill towns where they remain today— in Arezzo, Cortona, Montepulciano, Siena, and elsewhere—as powerful reminders of the end of freedom. Like their Etruscan and Umbrian ancestors, the citizens of the hill towns were so insular and so proud of their individual cities that they permitted themselves only temporary alliances against a common enemy. The towns were, in fact, destroyed by the bonds that would have given them the strength to withstand outside invaders.

With their freedom gone, the creative impulses of the hill towns suffered, but the towns themselves survive as architectural compositions of light and shadow, stone and brick. To Bernard Rudofsky they are among "architecture's nobility," for they are built to the measure of man and formed by the rhythms and traditions of a satisfying life. Even on their intimate scale, these towns are every bit as densely built as our own cities, yet they engage our emotions and excite us with their sensuous and aesthetic pleasures. Everywhere we look, the centuries are piled up one on top of another: Etruscan wall next to Roman gate next to medieval duomo and Renaissance palazzo. People are born, married, and buried in the same buildings and spaces as their ancestors, and share the ceremonies of daily life in the piazze that are the heart of the cities. The free-wheeling streets, the sculpted runs of stairs, the maze of tiny alleys and narrow lanes that are the capillaries of city life, the brush of green in a single tree, arcades reaching over streets like canopies of stone, and wooden loggias all create a rich and sensuous texture that stirs the emotions and inspires a sense of the civilizing effect of these harmonious hill towns.

Italians have made a great success of living together in cities because they derive from them an immediate source of pleasure and identity. Within the city, the street is home, and women lean out of shuttered windows and look down onto the streets below. Indoors they inhabit a mysterious darkness that few foreigners ever penetrate, but the windows become their eyes on the world, dividing dark interiors from the brilliant world outside. William Hazlitt, the English writer, couldn't bring himself to approve of this "prurience of the optic nerve," the willingness Italians have to take in everything through their eyes, but it is part of the warmth and the sense of involvement and community that draw us to the hill towns. The street and piazza become shared public space, the focus of life, where the community gathers to talk and do business, where the town market spills its provender under canvas awnings and umbrellas, brilliant colors undulating like waves in a great stone sea.

Many travelers who came to the hill towns before the middle of the nineteenth century did so merely because they were obliged to stop somewhere along the way between Florence and Rome. They complained bitterly of dirty inns and appalling food, of dodging highwaymen and robbers, and of being cheated by carriage drivers. Montaigne, who visited Umbria in 1580 and 1581, reported in *Journal du Voyage* that the inns were drafty and uncomfortable, since there wasn't a pane of glass in Italy and the wooden shutters that kept out the wind also effectively shut out the light. Nearly two hundred years later, Tobias Smollett, as reported in *Travels Through France and Italy*, found the inns in the Umbrian countryside "abominably nasty, and generally destitute of provision; where eatables were found we were almost poisoned by their cookery; their beds were without bedcurtains or bedstead, and their windows without glass"; elsewhere, the bedclothes were enough "to turn the stomach of muleteer and the victuals cooked in such a manner that even a Hottentot could not have beheld them without loathing." At the beginning of the nineteenth century, Hazlitt wrote *In Notes of a Journey Through France and Italy* that he was appalled by carriage drivers, "vetturini who bargain to provide you for a certain sum and then billet you for as little as they can upon the innkeepers . . . who consider you as common property or prey, receive you with incivility, keep out of the way, will not deign you an answer, stint you in the quantity of your provisions, poison you by the quality, order you in their worst apartments, force other people into the same room or even bed with you, keep you in a state of continual irritation and annoyance all the time you are in the house." If these weren't problems enough, travelers had to endure passing through customs posts and changing money at each provincial border, since Italy remained a collection of regions until its unification in 1860.

The principal routes to Rome took travelers through Tuscany by way of Siena, or into Umbria from Venice to Rimini on the Adriatic. Many went by sea from Livorno to Civitavecchia, then traveled inland to Rome, missing the heart of Tuscany and Umbria altogether. There were inns at Radicofani, Acquapendente, and Buonconvento, hill towns that are rarely visited today but were then the conventional stopping places for travelers. Even those who spent weeks in Florence and traveled to Siena neglected to drive the few extra miles to San Gimignano, and Orvieto was merely a footnote to eighteenth-century guidebooks. In Umbria, visitors almost always headed for the falls at Terni and the springs of Clitunno, which were mentioned often in classical literature.

Most writers of travel books in the sixteenth and seventeenth centuries were ambivalent about Italy and warned of its dangers to the tourist's moral and spiritual life. Northern Europeans found the sensuousness of Italy intoxicating—its food, wine, and sunshine, as well as its ruins and dazzling landscape—for it was not only the lure of civility and the painting and sculpture that attracted them. Samuel Johnson, who never reached the shores of the Mediterranean, once said that "a man who has not been in Italy is always conscious of an inferiority, for his not having seen what is expected a man to see." Travelers obviously agreed and kept coming. By the eighteenth century, when there was scarcely an Englishman of fortune who was not dashing off to see the Continent, visitors were interested only in the country's classical past and its late-Renaissance revival, and many made patronizing comments about Gothic art and architecture. Confronted with the cathedral at Siena, Joseph Addison could only observe in *Remarks on Several Parts of Italy in the Years 1701, 1702, 1703,* "When a Man sees the prodigious Pains and Expense that our Forefathers have been at in these barbarous Buildings, one cannot but fancy to himself what Miracles of Architecture they would have left us, had they only been instructed in the right way."

The indifference to Italy's medieval past was due partially to a pronounced antipathy to her religion, and a sympathetic understanding of the Middle Ages had to await the eloquence of such writers as John Addington Symonds and especially John Ruskin, whose books created a taste for medieval art and architecture. Influenced by these writings, travelers began to stop in Orvieto and Perugia—places said by previous guidebook writers to have few objects of interest—and Tuscany became like a second home to many Englishmen. Henry James, a passionate traveler, returned to Italy time and again for "a deep delicious bath of medievalism," and William Dean Howells, who was United States consul in Venice for four years, became an enthusiast for Tuscan towns. Nathaniel Hawthorne, Charles Dickens, and Edith Wharton all wrote travel books charged with their deeply felt response to the country.

Tourism on a large scale really did not develop until the middle of the nineteenth century, after the advent of the railroad had made the Grand Tour obsolete. This heritage continues, and today we see the hill towns as romantic survivors of another era, as well as living presences in the modern Italian landscape. Today the hill towns are being discovered once again as unspoiled places somewhat off the familiar road between Florence and Rome. The food and restaurants are wonderful, the wine always abundant and in some cases startlingly fine, and handsome old buildings have been converted to hotels and pensioni.

In an introduction to Goethe's *Italian Journey,* W. H. Auden asked, "Is there any other country in Europe where the character of the people seems to have been so little affected by political and technological change?" Centuries of urbanity resonate within the brick and stone of all the hill towns, and their romantic power coupled with the celebration of life and history charges them with an energy and timelessness that call to travelers across the ages.

In courtyard, Upper Basilica of St. Francis, Assisi

17

Interior of Abbey of St. Antimo, Montalcino

18

Tuscany

Tuscany, with Umbria, forms the heartland of Italy. It is bordered on the west by the waters of the Tyrrhenian Sea; to the north and northeast, the Apennine chain encircles it like the embrace of a gigantic arm. Falling away from the mountains are a parallel series of smaller ridges that divide the region into protected valleys, each cut through by the pale ribbon of a stream. Of all these numerous rivers, only the Arno is of any size, although others, such as the Ombrone and Serchio, the Sieve and Era and Elsa and Arbia, wind through the landscape as they do through the paintings of Fra Angelico and Piero della Francesca. In this region the civilization of Italy was born twice, once in Etruscan times and once again, two thousand years later, when the Tuscans built the cities and towns that shaped their countryside. This is the image of Italy we carry in our minds: the rows of grapevines stretched in garlands between mulberries and elms; the silvery olive trees; the plots of wheat; the hills wooded with beech, chestnut, spruce, and oak; villa walls stained with soft pastels and rich earth tones; stone villages with castles and towers at the tops of hills; farmhouses whose dusty red tile roofs are set off by the dark flames of cypresses.

Tuscany's size—as the third largest region of mainland Italy—its setting at the center of the country, and the variety of its landscape have given it importance from the very beginning. The famous Tuscan farmland, with its serried rows of neatly pruned vines, olives, and orchards, looks almost unchanged from the frescoes of Fra Angelico, Benozzo Gozzoli, and the Lorenzetti, but it was painstakingly wrested from hilly, rocky soil by people who spaded and tilled it by hand, breaking the stones and setting them out in terraces. This careful marriage of man and nature makes much of Tuscany look like a garden, with harmonious towns set in an intimately scaled landscape. It was shaped, like so many of the world's most fertile areas, by water, and in Pliocene times was in fact contained like an inland sea by the Apennine range. Now, although many parts are familiar from the backgrounds of Renaissance paintings, this is a landscape of enormous variety, but no matter where its hill towns are set—rising above deep green folds of valley, sitting on an imposing tongue of land, or crowning the steep rise of a hill—they are part of a countryside carefully commanded by man.

The valleys of this countryside are among the most beautiful in the world. South of Florence, the Val d'Arno stretches from steep mountains with little stone forts and castles to lower hills thick with villas, terraced with vines and olive trees and dotted with poplars whose trunks are dark with climbing ivy. In the cool shaded forest high above the Arno lies Vallombrosa, famous since medieval times as a religious retreat. Little remains of the Benedictine monastery that was founded here by one of the many religious extremists of medieval Tuscany; instead it is most frequently visited nowadays by Florentines who make their way up the cool slopes to escape the oppressive heat of summer. Milton evoked the scene in *Paradise Lost* when he wrote of

> . . . *angel forms, who lay entranced*
> *Thick as autumnal leaves that strow the brooks*
> *In Vallombrosa, where the Etrurian shades*
> *High over-arched embower . . .*

The golden leaves of the great beech woods have actually become more numerous since Milton, because of the forty thousand trees that were planted here by the monks a century after the poem was written.

The valley of the mountainous Mugello, with its squares of farmland, its vineyards and orchards and long knots of hills, is set in the low wooded mountains north of Florence. Here the Medici built some of their farm-house villas: Cosimo I spent his youth at Il Trebbiolo, and the stout-walled Caffagiolo, originally a Florentine fortress, was home to many Medici as a summer resort. Fiesole, the hill town that is the mother of Florence, rises above the olive trees of the valley and the domes and towers of Florence itself. Late in the afternoon, when those domes and towers catch the pink light of the setting sun, and the stone walls are still warm to the touch, the view appears hardly changed since Shelley, quoted by Harold Acton in *Florence*, wrote of it; although of course, the air of Florence is no longer "smokeless":

> *You see below, Florence, a smokeless city, its domes and spires occupying the vale; and beyond to the right, the Apennines, whose base extends even to the walls. The green valleys of these mountains, which gently enfold themselves upon the plain, and the intervening hills covered with vineyards and olive orchards, are occupied by the villas, which are, as it were another city, a Babylon of palaces and gardens. In the midst of the picture rolls the Arno, through woods and bounded by the aerial snow and summits of the Lucchese Apennines. On the left, a mag-nificent buttress of lofty, craggy hills juts out in many shapes over a lovely vale, and approaches the walls of the city. Cascine is seen at intervals, the ethereal mountain line heavy with snow. The vale below is covered with cypress groups, whose obeliskine forms of intense green pierce the grey shadow of the hill that overhangs them. The cypresses, too, of this garden form a magnificent fore-ground of accumulated verdure; pyramids of dark leaves and shining cones rising out of the mass, beneath which are cut, like caverns, recesses which conduct into walks. The Cathedral, with its marble Campanile, and the domes and spires of Florence, are at our feet.*

When the Etruscans founded a city here at Fiesole, Florence was a mere ford on the Arno, for the plain held no attraction for the builders of a civilization whose cities were set on hillsides with crystalline air and far-reaching views. All that remains of Etruscan Fiesole, and the temple around which it was sited, is a few foundations. But huge stones from the ancient walls are still visible beneath the growth of ivy, and the excavated remains of the Roman bath and theater give some sense of the ordered plan the city must once have followed.

Hannibal started out from here on his destructive march through Tuscany, and Totila visited his savagery upon it; but what had once been a temple of Bacchus remained standing, to be transformed into the beautiful church of Sant' Alessandro when Theodoric the Goth came to Fiesole in the sixth century. The nearby Badia is another survivor, for the inset in its façade preserves a bit of the Romanesque original, like a fine old jewel in a rough, unfinished setting. Its diamonds, starbursts, arrows, lozenges, and wavy liquid lines are reminiscent of San Miniato al Monte in Florence, although here the tiny green and white marble designs are so delicate they might have been cut from fine paper like valentine designs. Fiesole's narrow lanes, bounded by walls on either side, open out to a view of the bowl of the Florentine valley and to the countryside, its green interrupted here and there by the dusty terra-cotta roof of a farmhouse or villa and by the measured geometrical layout of elegantly conceived gardens.

The great mountain massif of the Pratomagno rises between the valleys of the Arno and the Casentino, where the young Arno begins its reed-fringed voyage. St. Francis of Assisi received the stigmata at La Verna, the most sacred of Tuscan shrines, and Dante, who spent some of his exile in the Casentino, wrote of its green woods and valley. It remains covered with dense forests of fir, beech, and chestnut, and the pigs of the

Sorano

valley are still herded into the hills to feed on the beechnuts—a diet that contributes to the delicious flavor of the local hams and salamis. Deep within forests of fir are the shrines of Camaldoli, home of an ascetic order of monks founded in 1012 by St. Romualdo; the tradition is carried on today by white-robed monks who have taken a vow of silence. Lorenzo de' Medici and his Platonic Academy met here, and although the hermitage remains, the dense forest around it with its rich undergrowth of golden moss, wild cyclamen, broom, and fern was seriously damaged by trucks and bulldozers during World War II, when many trees were felled to form bridges for an offensive across the Po.

Midway between Florence and Arezzo the stone-arcaded hill of Poppi is crowned by a medieval Palazzo Pretorio with a perfectly preserved merloned tower. It was built for the Guidi family, who were among the major feudal overlords of Tuscany, by Arnolfo di Cambio, and has an unmistakable resemblance to the Palazzo della Signoria in Florence. Its battlements offer a perfect view of the field of Campaldino, where the Florentines were assured of dominance over Tuscany by the defeat of Arezzo in 1289. Dante took part in the battle and spent some of his life in exile with the Guidi. Indeed, it was from this castle that he wrote an impassioned letter to Emperor Henry VII, hoping he would wrest Florence from the administration that had exiled the Medici permanently. Dante addressed him as "the Bridegroom of Italy and the Solace of the World," and urged him "to come to Italy and enforce the peace and hew the rebellious Florentines like Agag, in pieces before the Lord."

Next to the Casentino, at the eastern edge of Tuscany, runs the narrow Val Tiberina. Rising above it are vast woods of sycamore, oak, chestnut, and fir. There are no major towns here, and in some sections it is rare to see a house or hear the barking of a dog. Overlooking the valley is the little town of Sansepolcro, the birthplace of Piero della Francesca; it was here that Aldous Huxley went when he announced that he was going to see the most beautiful picture in the world, the *Resurrection* of Piero, which remains in the Palazzo Comunale.

Extending from Arezzo past Cortona to Chiusi and skirting Lake Trasimeno, which is just across the border in Umbria, is the narrow Val di Chiana. Once known as the "granary of Etruria," it reverted to intractable marsh in the Middle Ages and has only been thoroughly reclaimed in the last hundred years. Today, along with orchards, vineyards, and olive trees, fields of sugar beets, corn, and tobacco form a patchwork across the intensely cultivated landscape, and the powerful white Chianina cattle that are the source of the famous *bistecca alla fiorentina* still appear in the farmlands.

Chiusi, the most important city in the Etruscan kingdom, sat high on its densely wooded hillside at the southern edge of the Val di Chiana, where it rose above the morning mists that still flood the valley, leaving hill towns like islands in a great white sea. After the legendary ride of the great Etruscan king Lars Porsena, the power of Chiusi began to ebb. Seven centuries of Etruscan art remain in the museum as testimony to the city's creativity, but while there is no trace of the monumental tomb of Porsena that Pliny described in detail, two painted tombs under the hill are rich in architectural and decorative detail.

The Romans named the city Clusium when they made it a military colony; the Goths used it as a staging post to fight Belisarius; the Lombards settled it as a capital; and the cities of Orvieto, Perugia, and Siena all fought to conquer it. Now the signs of the past are visible in the early Christian basilica that became the medieval Duomo and in the square Lombard tower and later chunk of campanile that overlook narrow medieval streets.

Following the curve of the Apennines to the southern reaches of Tuscany we come to Monte Amiata, Tuscany's single volcanic cone of a mountain, to the west of which the land takes on a darkly tawny hue. Volcanic eruptions produced the cliffs of tufa on which the medieval towns ride like ships above a sea of vegetation. At Pitigliano, tall houses are set along the edge of a precipice "like teeth in a jaw" above a dense growth of ilex and shrubs. The porous red-brown earth at its base is pierced with hundreds of Etruscan tombs and with caves that have long served as a storage place for the wines produced in the region. From the fourteenth century to the last war, the little agricultural community of Pitigliano was the home of a sizable settlement of Jews who had found safe haven in the south of Tuscany, on the border of the Papal States. Nearby Sorano's steep-sided walls are similarly perforated with Etruscan tombs and Roman caves. A dense medieval town, Sorano has steep narrow streets that twist and turn as they wind up to the castle, although some parts of the city have crumbled away and are no longer accessible. Sovana, a third tiny nearby town with a single street, was known to be the birthplace of the papal reformer Pope Gregory VII, but its significant Etruscan remains had been abandoned and considered mere trifles by the inhabitants until a persistent nineteenth-century scholar came upon their remains in a tangle of underbrush.

From cliffs honeycombed with tombs and caves, the Tuscan landscape slopes toward the coastal plain of the Maremma, where, it was once said, "a man can grow rich in a year but becomes a corpse in six months." Although the Etruscans and Romans initially knew it as a fertile area planted with fruit trees and grain, by the end of the empire it had silted up and become a wasteland that turned to marsh and swamp, and by Dante's time it was infamous as the haunt of the deadly fever that was long attributed to breathing bad air and was thus known as malaria. The Maremma runs between the foothills of Monte Amiata and the Tyrrhenian Sea, forming a coastal plain where the Etruscans settled to mine the ores of the Colline Metallifere, the "metal-bearing hills," and the offshore island of Elba, and to build their cities of Vetulonia, Populonia, Rusellae, Cusi, Saturnia, and Vulci. Later the barbarians and the Saracens plundered it and passed on, and while the medieval cities of Massa Marittima and Grosseto prospered, it was only in the nineteenth century that the agricultural land of the Maremma was reclaimed by the dukes of the house of Lorraine, who ruled Tuscany after the Medici. It is now a region of pine woods, fertile fields, and vast estates, where cattle and sheep are grazed, although some of its strange primitive beauty still remains, as water buffalo, wild boar, and game inhabit its pasturage and thickets of thornbushes and herbs still grow in wild tangles. To the north lies Volterra, which looks to the plain of Lucca and Pisa, the coastal towns and white sandy beaches of Viareggio and Forte dei Marmi, and the port of Livorno.

Tuscany's abundance of natural resources includes mercury from Monte Amiata and mineral ores from the coastal mountains of the north, where in addition to deposits of salt, the geysers there provide borax and the trapped vapors are used to generate thermal electricity at Larderello. From the jagged Apuan Alps comes the famous marble of Carrara. The Apennines and the foothills of Tuscany are the source of building materials that have given the hill towns their distinctive character: dark green marble from Prato, the famous white from Carrara, pink from Siena, red from Roccalbegna, as well as other veined and colored marbles, the ubiquitous dull gray-brown sandstone, *pietra serena* from the hills of Fiesole and the blue-gray *panchina* of Volterra. The first great achievements of Tuscan art are the striped marble Romanesque churches of the Pisans, those mariners of the coast whose ships sailed for the distant East. They brought back spices and perfumes along with the bold black and white horizontal bands that spread their oriental mystery across Tuscany, reaching as far as the cathedral at Siena and the Baptistery at Volterra.

No landscape is more quintessentially Tuscan than the rich Chianti region, which extends from the craggy wooded hills near Florence to the low clay hills of Siena. The cracked chalky earth around Siena looks as bleak as a lunar landscape much of the year, but its surprisingly fertile soil, layered with limestone and flint, produces wheat, olives, and wines, the triumvirate that forms the diet of Italy. From the Chianti countryside come the olives for some of the world's finest olive oils, and the four types of grapes that are blended to become Chianti. Italy's most famous wine is the product of two types of red grapes—*sangiovese* and *canaiolo*—and two varieties of white—*trebbiano* and *malvasia*—and the numerous zones within the larger countryside produce an enormous variation in the floweriness, fragrance, and flavor of the individual Chiantis. The little hilltop towns dotting the area are relics of a time of fierce warfare when each noble had his own tower and walled fortress and when the villas were scattered among them, many now occupied by wealthy industrialists and foreigners, were fortified country houses, the original medieval outposts of the lords of the land. Here and there farmhouses are guarded by clumps of cypress and brightened by potted geraniums, where families still make their own prosciutto, salami, and cheeses and press their own rich green olive oil. The agricultural economy that characterized the countryside for centuries was interrupted twice, first by the barbarian invasions and later by the medieval warfare between Florence and Siena when the area's barons joined the Lega del Chianti to protect their interests. The symbol of the military association survives in the *gallo nero* (black rooster), emblem of the largest Chianti Classico consortium in Italy. The oldest winery in the area is the home of Chianti Brolio, where vines were grown and tended as long ago as the year 1000, but only since the peace brought by Grand Duke Cosimo I has the fortress of the Ricasoli family served uninterruptedly as a winery. It was Bettino Ricasoli, the "Iron Baron" who was Prime Minister after Cavour, who devised the formula from which Chianti has been made ever since. Once, as in every other vineyard in the farmland of Tuscany, the

In the Piazza del Campo, Siena

Ricasoli vines were linked like garlands to fig, elm, or mulberry trees and grew above rectangles of grain, filtering sunlight and screening the wind in a delicately balanced economy. But the modern world has intruded here, as in Umbria, and now almost all vineyards are being planted as a single crop and are cultivated and harvested by machine. Entire hillsides have become marching rows of vines, like soldiers conquering the countryside, and it is only in rare instances that both kinds of planting are still to be seen.

The Ricasoli winery at Brolio is but one of the many Chianti wineries in the gentle, rolling hill country where other producers bear aristocratic names like Frescobaldi, Serristori, and Antinori. Towns like Castellina in Chianti and Radda in Chianti sit on hills with fragments of medieval wall and castle, while Monteriggione crowns the top of a low hill with its perfect circle of a wall bristling with towers that once

rose much higher, like the giants to whom Dante compared them. Not far away, Colle di Val d'Elsa sits off the road to Volterra, on the ridge of a hill split into two parts connected by a bridge. The fame of the city dates chiefly from 1269, when it was the site of the battle in which the Florentines avenged their defeat at Montaperti and vanquished the Sienese, and with them the hopes of the Ghibellines in Tuscany. Colle Bassa, the lower town, looks essentially modern, although older structures still stand in the midst of the brick and putty-colored factories and commercial buildings. Colle Alta, the walled upper city, is medieval in great part. A monumental gate of brick and stone, with two cylindrical towers, is just wide enough to allow a single car to enter the town's only thoroughfare. Among the fine tower houses that line the street is the birthplace of the Florentine architect Arnolfo di Cambio, but for all its medieval ambience, a bit of Renaissance rustication and mannerist flourish touches the façades of the buildings, and Medici shields are reminders of the city's ultimate fate. Today the upper town is a quiet place, where old women knit in tiny piazze and men relax in *caffès* or wander down narrow passageways to the ramparts for a view of the Elsa winding below, past hillsides covered with olive groves. To the north Boccaccio's red brick town of Certaldo Alto still stretches along its hilltop with medieval towers and palazzi.

South of Siena stand now almost forgotten hill towns like Buonconvento, where Dante's Emperor Henry VII died. They are set along the Via Francigena, the great medieval highway opened by the Franks in the Dark Ages, which became a major route to Rome when the Val di Chiana reverted to marsh. Until the nineteenth century it was the thoroughfare exclusively used by travelers, and the small hill towns along it held the coaching stops and inns where they stayed.

Just beyond Buonconvento, the red brick Benedictine abbey of Monte Oliveto Maggiore rises on an isolated spur of land. It was established in 1313 in this solitary, harsh landscape by Bernardo Tolomei, a wealthy young Sienese noble who forsook the world with two friends; within a few years they found themselves with so many followers that the Pope granted them permission to become a Benedictine order. The monks made the pale gray earth bloom and turned it into a green oasis in the barren countryside. The walls of the cloister of the monastery were the first in Tuscany to be embellished with fine art when they were frescoed by Signorelli and Sodoma with scenes from the life of St. Benedict. Benedict, the father of Western monasticism, had great influence in Tuscany, where early monastic communities cultivated and reclaimed the landscape; they were followed in the Middle Ages by penitential men like Tolomei who established similar centers to preserve and transmit the highest values of the culture. All around Monte Oliveto Maggiore, the *crete*—infertile clay soils—are cracked and dry, with ruined bits of tower and castle on every hillside providing reminders of the days when the Aldobrandeschi nobles terrorized the countryside—they bragged they could sleep in a different castle each night of the year—and made travel in the region a precarious experience.

Montalcino, the last outpost of the territory controlled by the Sienese commune, is set on a hilltop among olive trees. Yellow-gray stone houses rise in tiers along streets that are crowned by a massive turreted fortress, while wine shops on a little two-level piazzetta sell bottles of the deep rich Brunello wines that are produced only in the immediate countryside. The Palazzo Pretorio hoists a spiky brick tower whose view southward overlooks the Romanesque abbey of Sant' Antimo, which is said to have been founded by Charlemagne. Rebuilt in 1188, it is one of the most beautiful churches in Tuscany, with three graceful choirs radiating from a single fine apse. Translucent walls and windows made of alabaster from nearby quarries admit a blaze of golden light, and carved capitals with griffins, eagles, and other mythological beasts are superb examples of the Romanesque stone carver's art. The other great abbey in Sienese territory, San Galgano, is a monumental Gothic church, a now roofless shell carpeted with grass, that remains touched with the French elegance of the Cistercian monks who brought the pointed Gothic arch to Siena when they built the church.

Monte Amiata dominates the landscape south of Siena, and although it appears variously soft blue or violet in the distance, it is in fact wooded with groves of chestnuts and beeches and forests of fir. A series of abundant springs flows from its porous rocks, gathering in pools where trout are abundant. Beyond the mountain rises the dark, brooding town of Radicofani, where the tower of a crumbling fortress presides over a barren height ringed by a few small houses separated by narrow, winding streets. The site was much fought over; the Lombards, the Popes, and the Sienese all wanted the protection of this scenic outpost, three thousand feet above the boundary between Tuscany and the old Papal States. Grand Duke Ferdinand I de' Medici built a hunting lodge here, which was transformed into a hotel described by John Evelyn in 1644 as "recommended for the refreshment of travellers in so inhospitable a place." The hotel has long since disappeared and visitors are rare here, although the forbidding, dark air of the city remains.

Along with the landscape for which it is famous, Tuscany gave Italy its literary language, when Dante chose to write *The Divine Comedy* not in Latin but in the Tuscan vernacular. He humanized the language and gave it immediacy by locating people and events in the familiar local geography. Tuscans have always been known for the classical purity of their language—expressions like *lingua toscana in bocca romana* confirm a widely held sentiment—and Siena in particular is famous for the elegance and softness of its speech. It is Florence, however, that is preeminent as the center of the rebirth of classical learning and of the humanist revival that followed, as well as of the great art that

Tuscany produced. Petrarch, one of the great poets of Italy, prepared the way for the Renaissance by bringing about a reconciliation of past and present. When the Medici came to power, Florence was free to turn energies that had long been concentrated on politics toward the wide cultural arena. Enthusiastic pride in its classical and pagan past, studies of Greek and Roman literature, and a new surge of artistic energy set it apart from every other city. Here Brunelleschi built his dome, the largest in the world, on top of the Duomo; Ghiberti set his brilliant golden doors in place; Donatello created the first freestanding nude since antiquity; and Masaccio, "Giotto born again," painted figures with inexpressibly moving dignity. Venus was born on Botticelli's half shell, and the Graces of Spring danced in luminous Tuscan meadows. Humanism and science were seen as part of an intellectual continuum, two filaments of the same thread, so that Galileo's telescope and Michelangelo's chisel were both artist's tools for ordering the world and giving it form. Many of the greatest artists of the Italian Renaissance came to Florence from the hill towns: Leonardo from Vinci, Mino da Fiesole from Poppi, Signorelli from Cortona, Piero della Francesca from Sansepolcro, and Arnolfo di Cambio from Colle di Val d'Elsa. And Florence in turn sent these artists and others across Italy, where they beautified churches and palazzi and scattered the seeds of the Renaissance. The clear sense of recognition most people experience in the Tuscan landscape comes from the Annunciations and Adorations of Fra Angelico, the Lorenzetti, Gozzoli, and others who painted Tuscan peasants in a Tuscan countryside, as biblical figures in the Judean wilderness.

Tucked away in the hill country outside Florence are walled Renaissance and baroque villas, their lawns, parterres, and labyrinthine box hedges entirely hidden from view. One of the earliest of these was the Villa Medici, commissioned by the elder Cosimo for his son Giovanni; in the time of Lorenzo il Magnifico, it became a center for scholars like Pico della Mirandola, Ficino, and Poliziano, who were devoted to Platonic studies. Settignano is the location of the imposing villa I Tatti, where the library and the paintings collected by Bernard Berenson are now part of the Harvard University Center for the Study of the Italian Renaissance. In the same little town, the elaborate formal gardens of the Renaissance Villa di Gamberaia include clipped allées, ponds, grottoes, and fountains. Its outdoor rooms are as elegantly organized as those in a great house. To the south, among hills covered with oak and pine, stands Montegufoni, an immense castle built as seven separate houses joined together around a tower and set among enormous baroque gardens. During World War II, when it was owned by Sir George Sitwell, father of the literary Sitwells, most of the artistic treasures of Florence's churches and museums were hidden here, lined around its courtyards and rooms, safe from British as well as German guns. Now, once again, it has resumed the character of a civilized country retreat.

"It has been said that the Tuscan countryside is a diluted town," writes Guido Piovene in *Unknown Tuscany*. "In the same way, one might say that something of the countryside has entered the city walls; a lot of this still remains. It is the continuous fabric common to these parts of the world where civilization has been both concentrated and diffused; the work of nature and man are mingled together, and can be distinguished, one from the other, only by degree; society and solitude are mutually complementary." By the nineteenth century, after the Napoleonic Wars, more and more travelers were coming to visit and some of them to stay, attracted by towns that remained almost unchanged from medieval and early Renaissance times. In some places the Tuscan landscape itself is like a medieval town, with chains of hills forming the natural barriers and valleys becoming the cultivated interior. Shelley, Leigh Hunt, Walter Savage Landor, and Swinburne came here to write, as, in this century, did E. M. Forster, D. H. Lawrence, Aldous Huxley, and Richard Aldington. Somerset Maugham was a regular visitor, as were the three Sitwells—Sir Osbert has chronicled his experiences at his father's villa, Montegufoni—and Harold Acton, who lived in the great villa La Pietra, outside Florence. Bernard Berenson held forth at I Tatti, Mabel Dodge at Villa Curonia, and Violet Paget wrote under the name Vernon Lee at Maiano. The waves of tourists have continued to come ever since, to explore cities virtually unchanged since Petrarch and Dante walked their streets within a landscape familiar from paintings by the Lorenzetti and Fra Angelico.

In front of shop, Volterra

Torre del Mangia, Siena

Lying along its hills like an inverted Y with a great arched gate at the foot of each leg, Siena is "the best preserved city of medieval Italy," as Bernard Berenson put it, "—a singular work of art, which has no equal in our western world." Its spiderweb of streets forms a tracery across hillsides with plunging drops of stairs, piazze faced with tall houses and beautiful Gothic churches, and fountains that are really deeply arcaded small houses of water. Old stone arches, towers that communicate across tight labyrinthine streets, stone animals on cornices and iron beasts to hold torches on ancient palaces, arched doorways, and raked angles of roofs sculpt their forms on this streetscape of precipitous falls and rises that seems as uneven as the land after an earthquake. It is all uphill and down, a city of rosy brick and gray travertine bumping up against the bold black and white stripes of cathedral and campanile, sunlight and shadow etched against a blue sky.

Of its Etruscan days no trace remains, and the forum, baths, and theater from Roman times are gone as well. Legend says that Siena was established by Senius, fleeing Rome after the death of his father, Remus. With his brother he set up the familiar Roman wolf suckling Romulus and Remus as the symbol of the city, and chose black and white for the shield,

because he rode a white horse and his brother a black one, or perhaps because the two of them were hidden from enemies by two clouds, one black and one white, as they made their way north to safety.

Siena became a Roman colony during the time of Augustus, but from the decline of empire through the Gothic invasions, a mysterious gap remains in its recorded history. Lombard kings were succeeded by the Franks, who gave Sienese nobles their ancestors and dotted the hillsides with castles from which they plundered the entire area. In the twelfth century, after forcing its barons within the city walls and limiting the secular powers of its bishops, Siena became a free commune and by the thirteenth century was internationally recognized as a major banking and commercial power. The commune and the prosperous merchant families expressed their civic pride by building great palazzi and churches and decorating them with frescoes by Duccio, Simone Martini, and the Lorenzetti brothers. When the great Ghibelline and Guelph conflict broke out in the early thirteenth century, Siena took the side of the Emperors, while her rival, Florence, a mere forty-five miles away, supported the Popes, and for three centuries the two fought for control of the countryside and its cities, for the road that led to Rome and the sea.

Siena sits on the old Via Francigena, which became the great medieval highway used by every emperor on his way to Rome, and while the city made the most of its site, it was essentially betrayed by nature, which gave it neither river nor outlet to the sea. Instead of commanding mountain passes as Florence does, Siena is left to overlook what was the swamp of the Maremma on one side and the clay hillsides of the southern Tuscan *crete* on another. Three centuries of stormy upheaval began in earnest with a Florentine ultimatum after the city took in Florence's Ghibellines, and the Sienese dedicated themselves to the Virgin before marching off in 1260 to the battle of Montaperti, where ten thousand Florentine soldiers were killed and another twenty-five thousand wounded—a sweeping victory that put the Ghibellines in control throughout Tuscany. The slaughter was so great, Dante wrote, that the waters of the nearby Arbia River ran red, but Siena rejoiced, and the victory cemented the city's dedication to the Virgin. The keys of the city were laid before her image in the Cathedral, and coins were struck with the phrase *Sena Vetus Civitas Virginis*—(Siena, the Ancient City of the Virgin). But nine years later at Colle di Val d'Elsa, the Florentines effectively buried the Ghibelline cause in Tuscany. Inside Siena, governments rose and fell, reflecting conflict between the merchants, the people, and the noble class, and the regimes of the Twenty-Four, Thirty-Six, and Fifteen were succeeded by the rule of the Nine, an oligarchy that held power from 1278 to 1355. These regimes were composed of multiples of three, and were controlled by citizens representing Siena's three sections—Città, Camollia, and San Martino, one for each of the ridges on which it stands—but the most dynamic of communal societies was that of the Nine, who presided over the city's golden age.

At the heart of this beautiful city is the Campo, the shell-shaped piazza set in the sloping hollow where the three hills of Siena meet. It is totally encircled by tall palazzi that undulate softly with its curves and enclose and protect it, so that it can be discovered only in slices of view that cut visual wedges down a ripple of stairs or funnel of street from the dark narrow arteries that are drawn to its elegant beauty. In the mists of the morning, leafy greens, translucent stalks of pale cardoons, and blazing red ovals of *pomodori* appear at the market that is set against the stone and pink brick of the great town hall, but as the sun blazes through the cool haze, fruits and vegetables are sold and carried off, and the market disappears. Laid out in 1195 and finished in 1346, the delicate hollowed cup of its center, where the Roman forum once stood, was always a theatrical backdrop for the life of the city. Montaigne thought it the "most beautiful portion of the city" the first time he visited Siena, in 1580, and on his return decided it was "the finest of any in the world." For more than six centuries it has been witness to the city's life. Knights always assembled here before going out to battle, and all of Siena came to celebrate the triumphant victory of Montaperti. Processions honoring Duccio's *Maestà*, destined for the Duomo altar, and the Fonte Gaia in the center of the Campo, serpentined around the fan-shaped hemisphere, and forty thousand people packed its core to hear St. Bernardino preach and fulminate against luxury, dissension, and gambling.

Henry James, in *Italian Hours,* described the Campo as "a bow in which the face of the Palazzo Pubblico forms the cord and everything else the arc." Its rosy-pink brick pavement is divided by strips of travertine that radiate like the striations of a seashell and divide it into nine parts, a tribute to the government under which it was paved. These ribs of gray stone converge downward, drawn to the centripetal force of the Palazzo Pubblico, the city's town hall and the most commanding building in the piazza. It dominates the space with the rhythms of its slightly curving wings, the ripple of its elegant tripartite Gothic windows, its open loggia, the little white outside chapel, and the extra-ordinary slender tower, perhaps the most beautiful in Italy, that rises with the aristocratic elegance of a lily and is named for the first bell ringer, an extravagant young man who was laughingly called Mangiaguadagni (one who eats his earnings, or spendthrift) and then shortened to Mangia ever after.

The Palazzo was originally the only building of the commune, and it began, in 1207, as a simple one-story barn with a wooden roof. Most city meetings were held in the nearby church of San Cristoforo, and everything else was rented—the prison, the city council rooms, even the bell tower whose bells called the populace to prayer or battle. Bricks and stones scavenged from other towers were transformed into two flanking three-story wings, finished by 1310; then a courtyard with a new prison and offices was added; and by 1341, the slender stalk of the tower rose, its crenellations numbering nine in honor of the rulers, its crest an elegant fillip devised by the painter Lippo Memmi. An external chapel commemorates the end of the plague that decimated Siena, reducing its population from one

We went off betimes, next morning, to see the Cathedral, which is wonderfully picturesque inside and out, especially the latter—also the marketplace, or great Piazza, which is a large square, with a great broken-nosed fountain in it: some quaint Gothic houses: and a high square brick tower: outside the top of which—a curious feature in such views in Italy—hangs an enormous bell. It is like a bit of Venice without the water.

CHARLES DICKENS
Pictures from Italy

hundred thousand to twenty thousand. This great civic building, the secular equivalent of the celebrated Cathedral, encapsulates the history of the city from its communal beginnings to the death of liberty that is spelled out in the coat of arms of Cosimo, the Medici duke who subjugated Siena in 1555 after a terrible siege. This began in 1554 and lasted for fifteen months, turning the countryside into a wilderness whose scarce trees "seemed to bear dead men," wrote a Spaniard; the bodies were those of Sienese who tried to bring provisions into the city. Mules, cats, rats, and the grass that grew at the walls' edges were the only available nourishment, and though they had sent away all the women and children and old people, the Sienese were forced to capitulate when people began to fall dead in the street. The black and white shield of the republican commune appears over every door and window, and at the top of the building, symbolic of the closeness of city and church, is St. Bernardino's blazing emblem of Christ, the mystical monogram of the letters YHS, surrounded by twelve rays that he sprinkled across the face of medieval Italy.

Once the walls and gates of the city had been built to make it strong against its enemies, the government turned to making the city beautiful and consciously concerned itself with aesthetic decisions. The ordered universe of theologians became the ideal for the city of man, and although the city grew organically, it was guided by rational plans and deliberate forethought. In Siena, a town planner called a "Judge of the Streets" ordained the uniform measurements for the width of the streets, mandated the brick paving that serpentines across its irregular surface, and decreed that all walls facing the street must be made of brick. When shoemakers and tailors put shops on the handsome Banchi di Sopra, the council of the city declared it "ruined" and decreed that trades must be grouped together in various parts of the city and that "within these boundaries no other tradesmen shall be able to set up." And even though the fourteenth-century city that still dances before our eyes in the churches, walls, and streets of Siena is an anonymous masterpiece by many hands, as much a result of organic growth as of rational planning, Siena's builders created a rich illustration of the ideas of later town planning enunciated by philosopher-architect Leon Battista Alberti in the fifteenth century. "Within the heart of the city," he wrote "it will be handsomer not to have the streets straight, but winding about."

Inside the Palazzo, Ambrogio Lorenzetti's frescoes of the *Effects of Good and Bad Government* give a fresh and enchanting picture of fourteenth-century Siena and its neighboring landscape. In the center of the city, merchants are at work in their shops and lovely young women are dancing in the streets, while out in the countryside, men are hawking and hunting and peasants are gleaning in their fields or bringing their animals and produce to town. Good Government is shown as a kindly old king dressed in the black and white of Siena attended by a number of Virtues, and Peace stretched out languidly on a multicolored bench, while in a corresponding picture of Bad Government the great horned devil of Tyranny is shown in the company of Avarice, Pride, and other vices.

The next room, the Sala del Mappamondo, contained a large map of the known world, since eroded to dust. Simone Martini's *Maestà*, the Madonna of the Court, sits on her gilded throne, surrounded by saints and angels against a sky as luminous and blue as lapis lazuli. Facing her is Martini's magnificent fresco of the victorious commander Guidoriccio da Fogliano, one of the first secular portraits painted in Italy. Man and horse, in a bold celebration of military power, are caparisoned in the same almost oriental pattern, in brilliant contrast to the stark land behind, where a lone captured castle stands on one hill, the Sienese camp on the other. Beyond this room, fragments of Jacopo della Quercia's sculptures for the Fonte Gaia are all that remain of the magnificent marble sculptures of the huge fountain in the Campo, named "gay" for the fifteen days of celebration that marked the arrival of the first reliable source of water in the center of this square. Now replicas have replaced the fourteenth-century originals, and the remade fountain sits in its original spot near the restaurants and cafés that draw the people of the city from early morning through the *passeggiata* and late into the night.

Siena is divided into seventeen *contrade,* or neighborhoods, each like a self-contained city within a city—with its own church and museum, its own government building and leader, its own songs, mottoes, symbols, and even its own patron saint. Ask a Sienese where he comes from and he'll answer with the name of his *contrada*—Eagle, Snail, Wave, Panther, Forest, Tortoise, Owl, Unicorn, Seashell, Ram, Tower, Caterpillar, Dragon, Giraffe, Hedgehog, She-Wolf, Goose, for allegiance to the *contrada* determines everything. Each is an extended family, the real focus of feeling and identity within the city, and passions run so high around Palio time that husbands and wives often separate and return to their original *contrade.*

As the day of the race draws nearer and the horses are selected for each *contrada,* there are trial runs at night. Suspense begins to mount with the running of the *prove,* trials or rehearsals for the real event, which have a kind of religious intensity. Each day the city is more crowded, the Campo thicker with spectators, more balconies are draped with banners and bold splashes of color. The jockeys in rehearsal clothes are cheered on by members of the retinues that follow them, singing *contrada* anthems and urging their horses on to victory. The identity of each *contrada* within the city becomes clearer as the time of the race draws near: the green and orange banners of the Selva (Forest), the rhinoceros under an oak tree, the green and red banner with a white goose for the Oca (Goose), the red and blue banners with a white owl with a crown all hang in their *contrade,* which touch on the Campo. Crowds gather for the blessing of the horse in the church of each *contrada,* built especially for this ceremony without side aisles and with few or no stairs so that it is easy, or at least feasible, to get the beast into the church. That the horse is blessed before the jockey indicates a degree of skepticism about human constancy in this ritual, which is marked by complex financial agreements that attempt to shape its outcome (hundreds of millions of lire change hands) and by secret agreements with jockeys and between jockeys, whose loyalty, since they are outsiders, is never a sure thing.

In the parade that precedes the actual event, files of men dressed in brilliant velvet costumes and Renaissance wigs—figures from a Gozzoli procession come to life for the day—walk by the zebra-striped Cathedral and squeeze down the ramped entrance to the Campo, with drums and horns playing in the background, and circle the Campo, a slow measured ceremony that is an elegant prelude to the no-holds-barred race that follows. "When at last the beginning of the procession appears and the great Sunta bell on top of the Mangia Tower and all the bells of Siena begin to clang, and the multitude begins to roar, we know what the noise was like in the Roman amphitheatre when the first lions bounded in," wrote Seán O'Faoláin in *A Summer in Italy.* He is one of the many writers who have been captivated by the Palio. One by one, groups from each *contrada* appear, dressed in brilliant medieval costumes and accompanied by trumpeters and drummers, captains and pages, horsemen and knights in tunics, small boys linked with loops of laurel leaves, and the flag wavers whose skill and grace have unmatched elegance. After each *contrada's alfieri* (ensign bearers) perform for the crowd, seventeen teams of flag boys perform together, with the emblems of their *contrade.* "They flap and wave them," marveled O'Faoláin, "fluttering and crackling this way and that way, passing them under their elbows and

behind their backs, in and out between their legs, ending up with the splendid trick called *sbandierata* when they throw them high in the air like flaming torches, one to the other, while the audience roars its frantic approval." And with the notes of the drummers and trumpeters vibrating on the air that is already throbbing with a barely contained delirium, the great painted wooden chariot, pulled by enormous slow white oxen, finally arrives, carrying the Palio itself, the silken flag of the Virgin that will be given to the winner, to be the pride and glory of the *contrada* forever.

There isn't a single inch of room on the Campo. Every seat in the bleachers is full when shade falls across the square in the golden light of sunset, and the Mangia Tower casts a shadow like the hand of a great sundial, and the horses at last appear, prancing stylishly to the starting line, leaping about while the jockeys grab their fearful *nerbi,* tough small whips they are more likely to use on each other than on their horses. Bang! The starter's torch meets the powder charge and the race is on as the entire crowd roars with frenzy. After less than two minutes of bareback horses and tough jockeys racing with abandon, it is suddenly over, and victorious *contrada* members stream onto the track, surround the horse, scoop up the jockey, shower him with hugs and kisses, and carry him off in triumph. Weeks later, at dinner in the *contrada,* beneath lights and overhead lanterns in the street that becomes a dining room, the horse will rest in the seat of honor, while in the neighborhood of losers—the *contrada* that came in second and the winner's enemies—all is darkness and silence.

Once the Palio itself has passed, it is possible to see the aristocratic palazzi that line the center of Siena, all brick, or brick and stone, with Gothic elegance in their three mullioned windows and ogival arches. From the Loggia della Mercanzia, the center of fifteenth-century commercial life, set just above the Campo, the main streets flow in three directions, but there are neither sidewalks nor cars, in this city given over to people. The Banchi di Sopra and Via di Città are thick with shops of fine leather, shoes, and silks, with bookshops—for Siena is an intellectual city—and with cafés serving the almond *ricciarelli* cookies and the fruit-studded *panforte* cake for which it is famous. The melody of the urban streetscape is as civilized and controlled as the Sienese themselves, although that civility covers a ferocity visible in the Palio and in the fierce allegiance the *contrade* demand. The Palazzo Tolomei, the oldest private palace in the city, a curtain of gray stone pierced with a screen of Gothic windows, stands near the Palazzo Salimbeni, a thirteenth-century palace with two adjoining golden Renaissance buildings that now form the preeminent Monte dei Paschi bank. Once the Tolomei and Salimbeni were fearful enemies—the Capulets and Montagues of Siena—and their palazzi bristled with their never-ending feuds, which were orchestrated with treacherous plots, riots, and murders. The other great merchant families built their palazzi along the streets that curve and wind within the city's heart. On the sinuous coil of the Via di Città, the Chigi-Saracini had a tower so high that the city drummer reported on the progress of the battle of Montaperti from it. Today, with a lone leafy tree against its silvery stone, it is an international music academy. When classes are not in session, it is possible to go upstairs to the collection of great paintings, which includes two Sassettas and a Botticelli. Across the street, the Palazzo Piccolomini delle Papesse, built for the sister of Pope Pius II, resembles other Renaissance palaces designed by Bernardo Rossellino with its rough rusticated lower stories, but it has Sienese details such as the elegant mullioned windows, forbidden in austere Florence, and a painted vault and stone well in the interior loggia. The other Palazzo Piccolomini in Siena is set at the edge of the Campo near the Università with its hundreds of foreign students. Behind the robust stone façade, also designed by Rossellino and very similar to his Piccolomini Palace in Pienza and Alberti's Rucellai Palace in Florence, on which he worked, is the State Archive, which contains all the usual documents pertaining to the affairs of state. Sixty thousand parchments in three rooms are history writ in treaties and papal bulls, in records of battles both successful and not, in the acceptance of Gian Galeazzo Visconti of Milan to help Siena out of a dilemma by becoming its Signoria (supreme magistrate), in the threats of Cesare Borgia to destroy the city, and in the records of the slow and ghastly siege of Siena by the Spanish in 1554 and '55 when its republican citizens were gradually starved into submission. The archive reflects the city's artistic life—a copy of Boccaccio's will is here, along with a manuscript copy of *The Divine Comedy*—in its most extraordinary collection, the Tavolette della Biccherna, which are the painted wooden covers of the city's account books. Siena's business life is documented in its ledgers and tax records, as is its history, since every six months, from the mid-thirteenth to the beginning of the seventeenth century, when a fresh set of registers was begun, the city's finest artists were commissioned to paint the covers. Both Lorenzetti, Taddeo di Bartolo, Sano di Pietro, Vecchietta, and Francesco di Giorgio Martini are included in the collection. From the windows of the palace is a glorious view down over the Campo. Nearby, the Palazzo Buonsignori, one of the most elegant Gothic buildings in Siena, has been transformed into the city museum. Almond-eyed madonnas, serried ranks of angels, Annunciations, and Crucifixions appear again and again in a display of more than three hundred paintings. They have the purity and single-mindedness of the Middle Ages—all gold paint, pinks, reds, and velvety blacks, and the blue of heaven for the Virgin's cloak—and they essentially comprise the total history of Sienese painting. Duccio, "the flower from whose seed all Sienese art sprang," according to Berenson, brought the drama of expression and linear grace to the art of painting. During the next generation, Pietro Lorenzetti's paintings exhibit a sense of body structure, and his brother Ambrogio's *A City by the Sea* and *A Castle on the Shore* are among the first pure landscape paintings in the history of art. With crenellated walls, pink and silvery-gray buildings, stalks of towers, and castles by the lake shores, these scenes are the first evocations of the ancient countryside as it actually looked and were painted purely for the pleasure of portraying it. Sassetta, "who lived and painted as if Florence were not forty but forty millions of miles away," according to Berenson, painted decorative and beautiful pictures, while other contemporary followers spanning the late fourteenth and early fifteenth century include Taddeo di Bartolo, who "caught a glow of splendor" from his predecessor, and Bartolo di Fredi, whose sumptuous paintings of fourteenth-century life with richly dressed kings and gentlemen are set against the hilly city of Siena and its countryside with processions of men on horseback. They give way to Vecchietta, Matteo di Giovanni, and Neroccio di Bartolomeo Landi— "Simone came to life again," says Berenson. Renaissance painting arrived in the sixteenth century with Sodoma, a follower of Leonardo, and Beccafumi, the mannerist, whom the eighteenth-century Italian art historian Luigi Lanzi called "the Caravaggio of middle Italy."

From the palazzi to the Duomo at the high point of the city, it is a sharp uphill climb. Alternating black and white bands wrap around the sides of the Cathedral, which rises on a site occupied first by a temple dedicated to Minerva and later by an early Christian church. The exuberantly zebra-striped emblem of fourteenth-century Siena grew slowly over a period of fifty years, and its façade, which began in Romanesque vocabulary, was increasingly inflected with a Gothic accent. On the lower part of the face of the Duomo, Giovanni Pisano formed three enormous round Romanesque arches, surrounded them with gables, pinnacles, and recessed bands with animal symbols, then sculpted prophets and saints who strain and turn away, animating the façade with dynamic energy. Above the lower section, in a Gothic design similar to Maitani's for Orvieto Cathedral, a circular rose window is set with a square frame and surrounded by three triangular gables aglow with golden mosaics. Henry James described the glittering detail of the façade as a "goldsmith's work in stone"—with white marble from Carrara, pink from Siena, and dark green from Prato—with sculptures on the sides and top standing in relief against the sky. Had the plans been carried out, this would have been a much larger cathedral than its rivals in Orvieto and Florence. But before work had gone far, the financial reverses of the 1340s, the devastation of the plague, and the weakness of columns too slender to support the gigantic structure brought the construction to a halt. Beside it, the campanile with its black and white stripes dominates the skyline.

Inside the Cathedral, a forest of clustered columns reaches high to ceiling vaults painted deep blue and sprinkled with golden stars. When Taine entered, he found the experience incomparable: "that of Saint Peter's in Rome does not approach it." Its mass of chapels, paintings, sculpture, choir stalls, and pavement are a collective expression of Sienese art that includes Nicola Pisano's octagonal pulpit, the Piccolomini altar with figures by Michelangelo and Bernini, Donatello's *John the Baptist,* Beccafumi's dancing angels, and inlaid wooden choir stalls that Henry James described as "the frost work on one's windowpane interpreted in polished oak." Pinturicchio's enchanting frescoes of Pope Pius II outline the life of a Renaissance hero from his days as a young man setting out in the world to his ascension to the papacy. The famous floor, an enormous carpet of inlaid colored marble designs, is like a gigantic book telling stories from the Bible. Domenico di Bartolo, Matteo di Giovanni, Beccafumi, and Pinturicchio were only a few of the artists who contributed to these elegant vignettes over a period of three centuries. The best of them are almost always hidden by protective wooden planks and are unveiled only from August 15 to September 15.

But the great treasure of the Duomo is the Cathedral Museum, where Duccio's *Maestà* is ensconced in a dark room of its own, the golden background of its rich forms glowing with a sumptuous warmth. Berenson calls Duccio "the last of the great artists of antiquity in contrast to Giotto, who was the first of the moderns," and here the slow movement of the heads of angels and saints, the elegance of line and jewel-like color are an epiphany of Byzantine and Gothic forms. On the day that the citizens carried it from the artist's workshop to the Duomo, shops were closed in Siena and bishops led a procession around the Campo and then to the altar of the Cathedral, where it was hung so that its scenes were visible from both sides.

Stairs circling the apse lead to the Baptistery, the church below the church, which is like a crypt in this city of many levels. Inside, among the vaults and pillars and frescoed walls, a massive font by Siena's greatest sculptor, Jacopo della Quercia, rises on a slender stem to an enormous full-blown form, with bas-reliefs by Donatello, Ghiberti, and della Quercia himself, the first Tuscan sculptors of the Quattrocento—the fifteenth century—who combined Gothic elegance with the humanism of the coming Renaissance. Angels are interspersed among the panels that tell the story of the life of John the Baptist in vignettes that include Donatello's depiction of the shattering moment when Herod is presented with the head of the shaggy prophet, an incident portrayed with such explosive force that its influence can be found in later artists, including Leonardo.

The Cathedral had a bewitching effect on Nathaniel Hawthorne, who went back to it time and again. He described the façade, in his *French and Italian Notebooks,* as "a magnificent eccentricity, an exuberant imaginative flowering out in stone," and called the Cathedral "a religion in itself—something worth dying for to those who have a hereditary interest in it." William Dean Howells was similarly moved. In *Tuscan Cities* he writes: "There are a few things in this world about whose grandeur one may keep silent with dignity and advantage, as St. Mark's, for instance, and Notre Dame, and Giotto's Tower, and the curve of the Arno at Pisa, and Niagara, and the cathedral at Siena."

From the Duomo, dark winding streets skirt the Via Galluzzo, where light washes through arched passages that are canopies of brick, and casts soft shadows as if in little chambers below. It is not far to the home of St. Catherine, who became the patron saint of Italy. She is one of the three major religious figures from this city of spirituality—Bernardo Tolomei, who established the nearby monastery of Monte Oliveto Maggiore, and St. Bernardino are the others—and she might still be wandering among the precipitous alleys, so unchanged does this section appear. By choice, part of her childhood was spent as a recluse with nothing but a stone pillow for her head, and Catherine, who had had visions and revelations at a young age, went nowhere except to the nearby church of San Domenico for three years until she decided to devote her life to the Church. When she saw that the Church needed purifying, she took it upon herself to do the job. During the plague, she looked after the sick in the hospital across from the Duomo, then plunged into the thick of Siena's complex political maelstrom, wrote letters to the King of France and the rulers of many communal regimes in Italy, urged nuns to besiege heaven with prayers, tried to make peace between Guelph and Ghibelline, and was determined to influence the policies of both Church and state. Fearful of nothing, she became a power in Siena, then went to Avignon, "city of corruption," to see Pope Gregory XI and plead with him to return the papal throne to Rome. She bombarded him with letters and later hectored kings and popes in the name of goodness. She died at the age of thirty-three.

Her house is preserved within the section where tanners and dyers once lived—the odors of the tanneries were said to have saved them from infection during the plague—near the enormous triple-arched Fonte Branda, the oldest of Siena's fountains. With its deep brick arches, crenellations, and ancient marble lions, it seems more like a reservoir or fortress than most fountains, perhaps because water was perpetually scarce in Siena.

Where the nearby hillside drops steeply away, the massive brickwork and enormous buttresses of San Domenico tower above every other structure. The black and white stripes of its interior link it to the Cathedral. St. Catherine's memory pervades it, and one chapel contains her shrunken, mummified head along with Sodoma's famous fresco showing her in a swoon. Another chapel has Andrea Vanni's portrait picturing her wrapped in black with a long-stemmed lily in her hand, and a long, sad, ethereal face. Near San Domenico, in the Via Casati, is the enormous fortress built by Grand Duke Cosimo de' Medici. This was the spot where the Sienese rebelled against the armies of the Spaniards and their Florentine allies who had come to occupy the city.

If San Domenico is permeated with memories of St. Catherine, San Francesco, rising on the city's opposite flank, belongs to St. Bernardino, the sharp-witted, realistic monk who refused a bishopric so as to be free to preach all over Italy. He built his own oratory within the shadow of the larger church, which is all black and white stripes, dappled with light and color and graced with paintings by Pietro and Ambrogio Lorenzetti. It is the most austere of Siena's mendicant churches. On the hill beyond it, St. Bernardino placed his Monastery of the Osservanza, headquarters of the sect of Franciscans, who observe St. Francis's strict rule of poverty. Though bombs destroyed it during World War II, it has been rebuilt and now houses a number of lively Della Robbia glazed terra-cottas.

Now people stroll on the ramparts of the city fortress or sample the wealth of Italian wines at the permanent *enoteca,* the city's wine museum, in the ten-acre citadel, and most have forgotten that these enormous ramparts with their cool paths were built by Cosimo I de' Medici when he conquered Siena and consolidated the region of Tuscany, which was effectively one of the great powers of sixteenth-century Europe.

Nearby, at the gate of the Porta Camollia, the motto of the city welcomes visitors: *Cor magis tibi Sena pandit* (Siena opens wider than her heart to you). Because Siena was on the post road, it drew many travelers. Montaigne, in the sixteenth century, was enthusiastic; Boswell, in the eighteenth century, wrote to Jean-Jacques Rousseau that "the Sienese dialect is the most agreeable in all of Italy. For me it was a continual melody." Of the multitude of Englishmen who made the Grand Tour in the early part of the nineteenth century, many wrote negatively of the Gothic style, which was considered barbarous at that time. By its end, a great reversal came about, largely effected by John Ruskin. Even as a very young man, when he went to Siena in 1840, he had written in his letters that "this town is worth 50 Florences." Liszt joined Wagner here and played a transcription of the third act of *Parsifal* while Wagner stood by the piano and sang along with him. The writers who came were numerous; they included the Brownings and Dickens, who called Siena "Venice without the water." Most of these nineteenth-century visitors make mention of the desolate quality of the city, which never recovered from the effects of the Spanish siege that left it with six thousand inhabitants instead of the previous forty thousand. Taine called it a "Pompeii of the Middle Ages," and Swinburne labeled it "Siena, the bride of solitude."

"Soft" Siena, which St. Bernardino excoriated for its luxury-loving ways, remains the welcoming city that left the stamp of its civilization on its painting, its rich golds and luminous color and line, and on the buildings that line its sinuous streets. The paintings have the same crystalline purity as the city's language, for the Sienese make art of everything they touch, and their city has the feel of eternity.

Early light, towers of San Gimignano

36

San Gimignano

Every day, buses and cars by the dozens wheel through the gentle Tuscan countryside, looping through the elegant geometry of carefully groomed olives and deep green vines on their way up to the city of the towers that floats like a dream image on the top of the hill. San Gimignano has preserved an authentic medieval skyline with its aggressive shafts of stone that make a sculpture of the city and the sky. Originally inhabited in Etruscan times, San Gimignano was named for the bishop of Modena who died here in 387, although one legend says that it takes its name from a local saint who saved it from destruction in the sixth century when he conjured up a supernatural vision that sent Totila fleeing in fear. The townspeople were so grateful, so the story goes, that they changed the name of the town from Castel della Selva (Fortress in the Woods) in his honor. The woods that once described the city have long since disappeared, to be replaced by the silvery olives and vines that march up to the gates of the city, softening its strong, stony look.

San Gimignano grew in beauty as well as size once it broke free of Volterra and became a free commune in 1199. Caught in the power struggles between Florence and Siena, it was a pawn in a game beyond its control and consistently ended up on the losing side, first Guelph with Florence at Montaperti, then Ghibelline with Siena for the fatal battle at Colle di Val d'Elsa. It was during a time of sustained crisis and constant violence that the city created the great medieval townscape that remains today, and if the creative energies that gave it its form were stilled when the Plague of 1348 devastated San Gimignano and broke its spirit, the bloody rivalry that raged out of control between the Guelph Ardinghelli and Ghibelline Salvucci was never interrupted. The two families built their towered fortresses next to their houses in the two great adjoining squares, and then began the savage battles and street brawls that affected the entire city as they loosed stones and arrows, burned the houses of their enemies, fought and killed and robbed, until they finally destroyed the city each side was determined to save for itself. San Gimignano was finally so exhausted by this civil war that it surrendered its liberty and in 1352

It did everything, on the occasion of that pilgrimage, that it was expected to do, presenting itself more or less in the guise of some rare silvery shell, washed up by the sea of time, cracked and battered and dishonoured, with its mutilated marks of adjustment to the extinct type of creature it once harboured figuring against the sky as maimed gesticulating arms flourished in protest against fate.

HENRY JAMES
Italian Hours

handed itself over to Florence, which built a fortress to stand as a reminder that the town's days of independence were over.

Today it is hard to visualize such passion and violence in this romantic town, which has preserved its medieval form in the honeyed amber of the past. A walk around the city, through the gate that pierces the wall at the Porta San Giovanni, past ceramics dealers displaying their plates hung on hooks in ancient buildings, past wine shops and butcher shops with pale white veal and fingers of fat sausages in neat glass cases, past knots of men collected on the steps of the great well in the piazza, and around the streets that climb and drop sharply, becoming staircases in the hill, such a stroll still takes less than an hour. It affords peeks down narrow winding streets and dark thin alleys that twist and turn and offer sudden vistas of the new roads and new houses and glances at the Tuscan countryside, lovely visions of civilized landscaping in which people have imposed their gentle patterns upon the earth, distributing cypresses and sowing wheat and corn in squares that dance up the hillsides, their golden color a counterpoint to the green of the vines.

As San Gimignano grew wealthy from silk and wool, artists came to paint frescoes, construct tombs, and ornament the architecture. By 1300, when Dante came as an emissary and asked the city to join Florence in the Guelph League, San Gimignano looked much as it is today, although of the approximately seventy-two towers that once crowded the hill, only fifteen remain, and some of those are abandoned, with moss and tufts of grass growing in the cracks. In the Piazza del Duomo, the Collegiata (or Cathedral), with stone steps as wide as the entire blank façade, has no great portal or glowing rose window, but inside its chaste shell its walls are a giant book of Sienese and Florentine art. Within the restrained black and white courses lining the arches, there are tortured scenes of betrayal and pain, vignettes of the wages of gluttony by Taddeo di Bartolo, and a St. Sebastian by Gozzoli. One wall is filled with Barna da Siena's frescoes of the New Testament, a complicated and densely organized series of scenes of violence, betrayal, perversity, and cruelty reflecting the emotional turbulence and disillusion of the period after the Plague. Directly across from them, Bartolo di Fredi frescoed the entire wall with scenes of the Old Testament, while Taddeo di Bartolo painted Judgment Day and the ghastly tortures of hell.

The Cathedral grew to its current size in the 1460s when the Renaissance architect Guiliano da Maiano added a choir, transept, and chapels, including the much admired one dedicated to St. Fina with its beautiful marble canopy by Benedetto da Maiano and the gold and white carved tomb. In it as well are a series of frescoes by Domenico Ghirlandaio depicting the life of Fina. The thirteenth-century virgin is supposed to have come home and told her mother that she accepted an orange from a stranger. The alarmed mother drew black pictures of what happens to little girls in such circumstances, and, overwhelmed by guilt, Fina felt obliged to humble herself and do penance for succumbing to temptation. She lay down upon an oaken board to repent and never rose again. When she died, it is said that the bells of San Gimignano rang spontaneously and violets began to bloom, perfuming not only the room that had become her perpetual bed, but the entire city as well. And yet St. Fina's city is the same city where Folgore da San Gimignano wrote his hedonistic verses celebrating the sybaritic life he and his friends lived, the same city that sprouted towers as monuments to arrogance, power, and greed, for violence and piety were inextricably mixed here.

Next to the Duomo rises the three-story Palazzo del Populo (Town Hall) with its adjacent great arched loggia, its double outside staircases, and its great tower, Torre Grossa, which rises 174 feet above the herringbone brick paving, marking the maximum height permitted to private buildings. Dante must have walked into the beautiful courtyard with its loggia, where justice was formerly administered, and climbed the staircase when he came to convince the priors to join the Tuscan Guelph League. It had just been finished then, in 1300, but the Lippo Memmi *Maestà* in the Sala del Consiglio was not here when he came, and was only finished more than a century later when Benozzo Gozzoli added three figures to it in 1467. The great high tower of the merloned palazzo looks at the neighboring campanile of the Cathedral, the only nonbelligerent tower in sight, and stands six feet higher than the one of Palazzo del Podestà, directly across the piazza. Even today a climb around the city walls, past houses with gardens where figs grow and lines of washing blow in the wind, past a single stone bench and down angled stairs, gives dramatic views of the towers

The hazy green of the olives rose up to its walls, and it seemed to float in isolation between trees and sky, like some fantastic ship city of a dream. Its color was brown, and it revealed not a single house—nothing but the narrow circle of the walls, and behind them seventeen towers—all that was left of the fifty-two that had filled the city in her prime. Some were only stumps, some were inclining stiffly to their fall, some were still erect, piercing like masts into the blue.

E. M. FORSTER
Where Angels Fear to Tread

San Gimignano

in the cityscape, although none is better than the climb behind the Cathedral to the crumbling Rocca, which Cosimo I destroyed.

Beyond the piazza, the Via San Matteo slices past the double towers of the Salvucci, protagonists of the medieval wars, past high stony tower houses and lower palazzi with elegant Sienese mullioned windows, with courts and loggia and a touch of color in the ubiquitous painted shutters. It curves slowly and sinuously until it reaches into the piazza where the Church of Sant' Agostino rises high on its stair. An unprepossessing exterior conceals the splendors inside, where, beneath a single nave and wooden trussed ceiling, Benozzo Gozzoli painted a charming series of frescoes of the life of St. Augustine, similar to those he painted of St. Francis in the little Umbrian town of Montefalco.

Although San Gimignano's towers are almost as famous as the Leaning Tower of Pisa, it was the rare traveler who visited them much before the middle of the nineteenth century. Until then the town was simply too far off the familiar route to entice visitors, who were, at any rate, interested in classical antiquity and the later Renaissance, and exhibited the taste of the age in their contempt for Gothic architecture and any painting predating Raphael.

One Sunday afternoon, on one of his many visits to Italy, Henry James succumbed to the pull of San Gimignano and left Siena for a visit. "The Tiny Town of Many Towers" not only satisfied his sense of the picturesque and romantic, but surprised him with its lively activity, and in *Italian Hours* James compared it to a buried hero waking up to show off his bones for a fee, and to a "sacred reliquary not so much rudely as familiarly and 'humorously' torn open." Edith Wharton first traveled to Italy as a child with her family, then returned year after year on her own. She loved to explore remote towns unknown to compilers of guidebooks and discovered a group of Della Robbia terra-cottas in an obscure Tuscan town, San Vivaldo, not far from San Gimignano, whose "fantastic towers," she wrote in *Italian Backgrounds,* "dominated each bend of the road like some persistent mirage of the desert." E. M. Forster made San Gimignano the model for his town of Monteriano in *Where Angels Fear to Tread,* on a trip that he said made him think of Italy as "the beautiful country where they say 'yes' and the place 'where things happen.'"

By the middle of this century, San Gimignano was so well known for its medieval beauty that many people were deeply upset by the erroneous report that the town had been destroyed during World War II. It in fact suffered severely, for the Germans discovered that the French were using the Palazzo del Podestà's high tower as an artillery post, and bombs sliced through a number of roofs and hit the Collegiata, damaging frescoes and walls. With great care the pieces were picked up and put back together again.

San Gimignano continues to attract visitors, who are lured by the romance of its towers and its elegant landscape. Along its streets there are new wine shops, and restaurants have opened their doors and hung out canvas awnings, and the old stones of ancient palazzi have been dusted and scrubbed for the new shops inserted within their old walls. Its Vernaccia wine, once praised by Michelangelo, is sold in great quantity, and the area is being heavily planted with vines to take advantage of its success. In the past the town was full of activity, its towers were in constant use, and its inhabitants scheming or listening to outsiders like Savonarola, who came to harangue the people with denunciations of sin before he went on to Florence in the fifteenth century. Now vitality has returned, and if its citizens are not exploding with the creative energy of the late Middle Ages, and the towers remain as ornaments, still the hush that lay across its stones has lifted and new life has come to San Gimignano.

Piazza della Cisterna, May Day, San Gimignano

Rising mists, Montepulciano

Perched and brown and queer and crooked,
and notable withal (which is what almost
any Tuscan city more easily than not
acquits herself of); all the while she may
on such occasions figure, when one looks
off from her to the end of dark street-
vistas or catches glimpses through high
arcades, some big, battered, blistered,
overladen, overmasted ship, swimming in a
violet sea.

HENRY JAMES
Italian Hours

42

Montepulciano

During the time of the harvest, the thick rich smell of grapes hangs in the air of the Tuscan countryside and pervades the Piazza Grande of Montepulciano. Trucks piled high with grapes from vineyards that are planted neatly on nearby slopes slowly climb the steep arc of the main street on their way to cellars dug out of the tufa of the city's volcanic soil. The seventeenth-century poet and physician Francesco Redi, in his *Bacchus in Tuscany,* called Vino Nobile di Montepulciano "the king of all wines," and travelers including Dickens and John Addington Symonds have agreed with his judgment. Nathaniel Hawthorne knew enough to call for a bottle of Vino Nobile to overcome the effects of a wine from Arezzo that he insisted tasted "as if it had tar and vinegar in it," but today one must hunt for an elegant ruby-colored Vino Nobile that lives up to its ancient reputation.

The city itself seems aloof from any controversy as it sits, somewhat reserved and withdrawn, on a hilltop that dominates the beautiful Val di Chiana at its narrowest point. Its main street serpentines along a narrow irregular ridge and splits to form a double backbone from which steep lanes drop precipitously downward, offering views into numerous little stone piazze or out over red-tiled roofs to valleys and rolling green hills sprinkled with cypresses, castles, and graceful umbrella pines. What Symonds called "the lordliest of Tuscan hill towns" is laid out upon a street that runs almost straight uphill and is lined with Renaissance buildings by Vignola, Sangallo, Peruzzi, and Scalza. It is they and the townscape itself that constitute the art of the city.

The city's fate is written in its geography. Of its prehistory we know little, but legend has it that when Etruscan kings ruled Rome, the city was formed as Mons Politicus by Lars Porsena, who made it his summer residence when the marshy air of Clusium (now Chiusi) became unbearable. The base of the façade of the Palazzo Buccelli, an assemblage of fragmented Etruscan urns and inscriptions, is sprinkled with prancing centaurs, winged horses, and stylized female figures from the city's earliest era. No mention of Montepulciano appears until A.D. 715, in the time of the Lombards, when it was known as Mons Politianus, but its location has always made it a rich prize. It crowns a hilltop two thousand feet above the sea, with a view over both Tuscany and Umbria that sees with perfect clarity the only pass where the ancient Via Francigena carves a path between the two mountains in the plain. On the morning after a storm has washed the sky and left only a few rags of cloud to cast fugitive shadows on the rolling land below, the air is cool and light, a fine antidote to steamy summer heat. From this enormous height above one of the great trade routes of Italy, Montepulciano was the inevitable site for a great fortress, but because it was neither rich nor powerful, the city became a prize contested by Florence and Siena and its history can be read in its political alliances.

For all its rich and complex past, Montepulciano is an exception among hill towns in preserving relatively little evidence of its medieval life. Most of its thirteenth- and fourteenth-century buildings were destroyed in fierce warfare when neighboring cities fought to control it and tyrannical families, hungry for power and wealth, unleashed savage battles within its walls. The city was faithful to nearby Siena until 1202, when it turned to Florence for protection, and continued to be shuttled between the two, with almost no voice in its own destiny, until early in the sixteenth century. When Siena captured Montepulciano in 1232, it was forced by the terms of the peace to pay for the total rebuilding of its dismantled defenses, and when the Sienese defeated the Florentines at Montaperti in 1260, one of its rewards was the return of Montepulciano, which had been wooed away by Orvieto in the meantime. The internal conflicts that forced the city to turn to strong outsiders were intensified in the fourteenth century when the powerful Pecora family became the rulers of Montepulciano and their battles, betrayals, and murders scarred the landscape.

And yet, for all its volatility in pursuing a changing course of protective alliances, Montepulciano remained faithful to Florence more often than not, and finally was permanently bound to that city in a pact prepared by Niccolò Machiavelli. When that occurred in 1512, Antonio da Sangallo the Elder was sent to rebuild the fortifications, which can still be seen at the great Porta al Prato at the city's northern entrance near the public gardens where cypresses and plane trees ring lawns edged in the springtime with tulips.

It seemed, in fact, an unknown world which lay beneath us in the early light. The hills, so definitely etched at midday, at sunset so softly modeled, had melted into a silver sea of which the farthest waves were indistinguishably merged in billows of luminous mist. Only the near foreground retained its precision of outline, and that too had assumed an air of unreality.

EDITH WHARTON
Italian Backgrounds

After Sangallo had finished his initial work, he sent for his son, Jacopo, and the architect Giacomo da Vignola to help. All along the streets, solemn façades of extraordinary buildings announce their origins in the fifteenth and sixteenth centuries, for Montepulciano is essentially a Renaissance city built by Florentine architects.

Edged by these monumental palazzi, the theatrical main street climbs and turns, tantalizing the eye and creating a sense of suspense with its serpentine curves. Here and there, on its almost vertical path to the Piazza Grande at the high point of the city, the street widens into piazze; the first is presided over by a column of the Marzocco, the Florentine lion, and the next, the Piazza Manin, by a clock where the familiar masked puppet in the Pulcinella clock tower beats out the hours. Children running up the hill at the end of the school day, feet slapping against the dark stone paving, invariably stop to watch as the minute hand approaches the top to see the figure raise an arm, turn, and hit the bell that chimes the time. Then, curiosity satisfied, they run on, passing white-tiled butcher shops that display entire sides of pork and the Chianina beef for which the area is famous, and numerous wine shops full of local specialties.

The street pauses in the piazza where the staircase rises to Michelozzo's Church of Sant' Agostino with a splendidly shaggy John the Baptist, tender Madonna, and St. Augustine crowning the lunette above the main portal. It continues in its path upward to the Piazza delle Erbe, where wheat was once sold in the loggia that bends elegantly with the arc of the road. When the sun penetrates the narrow canyons of this sinuous street, it warms the color of its weathered stone palazzi to muted tones of bronze, as golden as honey produced at farms in the neighboring countryside, and highlights their great rusticated façades and richly sculpted windows. The street continues relentlessly upward—past massive walls of stone with arched and pedimented windows and columns with Roman capitals, past a Sangallo palazzo sitting on a tiny piazza created by its wings, and past an unfinished Vignola with a great travertine door—until it curves around the crown of the hill like a great horseshoe.

As it swings past the modern re-creation of the Medici citadel with formal gardens of intricately planted hedges, it flattens out before arriving at the Piazza Grande, the gracious square shaped by the complex arrangement of its Renaissance buildings. Michelozzo's Palazzo Comunale, modeled on the

Palazzo della Signoria of Florence with its massive merloned tower thrusting high above the rough-hewn stones, rises on one side. Bold, severe, and aggressive, it appears as much fortress as city hall with its great form planted solidly across from two palazzi by Sangallo the elder. The view from here, obscured by the walls of buildings on every side, becomes apparent inside its plant-filled loggia or, even better, from the heights of its tower, for Tuscany spreads out over rivers and pale strands of streams, over the ashen land of the Val d'Orcia and the undulating hills and great green swatch of the Val di Chiana to the lonely volcanic mountain of Amiata, from Cortona and Lake Trasimeno into the soft hills of Umbria, over cornfields, green folds of valley, and hills with cypresses and olives, and forests of chestnut and beech as far as the eye can see.

Across from it, the weathered bricks of the façade of the Duomo, which is still waiting for the stone to cover its nakedness, stand next to the square tower, a rare medieval remnant of the original Romanesque church that crowned this hill. It gives no hint of the richness of its graceful light interior, with Taddeo di Bartolo's altarpiece ablaze with color, with pieces of Michelozzo's Aragazzi tomb, and with a Della Robbia altar. In summertime, when Montepulciano is the setting of the International Workshop of Music, chamber music floats over the tables that make the Piazza Grande an outdoor café, while the harmonies of violin and flute and larger musical ensembles fill the evening air. Once each year in August the piazza becomes a stage set as the elaborately costumed ritual of the Bruscello is performed by the townspeople. They create a theatrical pageant in song and verse centering on such legendary Tuscan figures as Pia dei Tolomei, Lars Porsena, and Catherine of Siena and on figures from such stories as Boccaccio's *Decameron*. In quieter times, groups of old men and women, all in black even to the hats and scarves that protect their heads from the fresh cool breezes, cross and recross the piazza, stopping to talk at the great well crowned by the Florentine lion and Medici arms. It sits off center, a little beyond the arcaded loggia of the nearest palazzo, a piece of architectural punctuation that gives balance and form to the buildings around its periphery.

Across from the Duomo, the Palazzo Nobili-Tarugi rises above its big arched loggia and opens toward the well of griffins and Florentine lions, while the Palazzo Contucci, with Peruzzi's baroque upper story, is set to the side of the Cathedral's campanile. In former days of power, Montepulciano's noble families

and church played host to Popes Clement VII, Paul III, and Julius III. Beyond the piazza, just over the crest of the hill, the sixteenth-century Palazzo Ricci of Peruzzi looks directly at the civic museum with its Sienese brick arches and an appealing small inner court. Inside are paintings possibly by Sodoma, Caravaggio, and Filippino Lippi, a fine Margaritone d'Arezzo portrait of St. Francis, and the town library of more than twenty thousand volumes, including various editions of the work of Angelo Ambrogini, known as Poliziano, the great Renaissance poet and scholar who was born and lived here before moving to Florence, where he became the resident humanist in the Medici household. The citizens of the town refer to themselves as Poliziani, not Montepulcianese, in honor of the Renaissance scholar.

Leave the central square on one side, and the street curves and dips sharply, with views over a hillside of occasional farmhouses and a landscape terraced with olives and neatly set vines. On the other side, the hill slides steeply away to the Teatro Poliziano, in whose open brickwork pigeons settle and nest.

For all its great distance from the valley floor, Montepulciano has long attracted visitors willing to endure the hardships of the ascent. John Addington Symonds is full of admonitions about the great journey up to its somber walls, and once there was more admiring of the view than of the town. Henry James wrote in *Italian Hours* that he had no consciousness of "what we were doing or what we expected to do, at Montepulciano. I think my reason must have been largely just in the beauty of the name (for could any beauty be greater?) reinforced no doubt by the fame of the local vintage and the sense of how we should quaff it on the spot. Perhaps, we quaffed it too constantly."

The art of the Renaissance permeates the city in the work of such Florentine architects as Michelozzo and Vignola, who collaborated with Michelangelo on the building of St. Peter's in Rome. It is visible as well in the magnificent Church of San Biagio, which is set in a green field just beyond the city gates on the shoulder of the hill. Built of blocks of travertine that have aged to a soft golden warmth, it was planned by Sangallo but finished after his death. Like Bramante's more ambitious plan for St. Peter's that was never built, it is a Greek cross in form, topped by a central dome and flanked by a freestanding campanile. The light-filled interior, with its classic columns, pilasters, and arches in harmonious balance, employs the forms of the ancient past and clearly exalts humankind in its new relationship both to them and to God.

Pienza

Pienza, an almost perfect early Renaissance town, was created by the will of a single man and built largely within a period of only three years. The town originally had the name of Corsignano, and although it is believed to date from Roman times, the few reminders of its previous history are a medieval gate, a Romanesque parish church, and the Gothic church of San Francesco. During the Middle Ages, the tiny village grew up around the nucleus of a small castle, which passed from the Abbey of Amiata to the Sienese family of the Piccolomini, who had estates in the vicinity.

It was here that Aeneas Silvius de Piccolomini was born in 1405. He grew up to be a humanist, a highly educated and literate Renaissance man, well versed in art, politics, and history. After he became Pope Pius II, he decided to transform his birthplace in hopes of making it a subsidiary papal court, and had it renamed Pienza in honor of himself. In 1459 he commissioned the Florentine architect Bernardo Rossellino to redesign his city, though Pius himself remained the controlling intelligence behind the project.

Pienza is still essentially one street, now called the Corso Rossellino, with a stupendous square, the Piazza Pio II, at its center. All the city's religious and civic buildings line its edges, but the square is dominated by the Palazzo Piccolomini, whose massive smoothly hewn walls, elegantly windowed façade, and colonnaded courtyard are quite probably modeled on the Rucellai Palace in Florence. which was built by Rossellino from a design by Leon Battista Alberti. Here the elegant inner courtyard is open to the sky, with a three-story arcade at the sides. It overlooks the hanging gardens at the back of the palace, with their neatly trained vines, clipped hedges, and dome-shaped trees.

Inside the palace, which had fallen into disuse and served as a granary in the nineteenth century but has since been restored, a broad staircase leads to rooms containing enormous fireplaces, richly painted wooden ceilings, fine old chests, and a red-velvet-curtained papal bed. Swords, cutlasses, and halberds cover the walls of one room, while incunabula, books, and papal bulls fill the impressive library. Just outside the palace

In Piazza Dante Alighieri, Pienza

is a wellhead of white travertine—the most copied of all Rossellino's works—whose classic round form, with stone columns rising above a circular stone base, is echoed by the travertine circle at the center of the square, which is the center of Pienza itself.

In his *Commentaries,* Pius wrote of consciously orienting his palace toward the volcanic cone of Monte Amiata, where in the summertime he convened his cardinals under the shade of chestnut trees. In taking advantage of the view he was following such classical writers as Pliny the Younger, whose villa near Città di Castello was built for its sunny southern exposure, with a carefully planned outlook over the Apennines. Rossellino's Duomo, on the south side of the square, is really a double church, with baptistery below and cathedral above, and with a pointed campanile rising high above the town. Outside, the inspiration is pure Alberti; inside, traces of Gothic blend with the grace of Austrian *Hallenkirchen* that had so captivated the Pope on his travels that he instructed Rossellino to copy their form. Light streams into a serene white interior, illuminating the chapels and works by such Sienese masters as Matteo di Giovanni and Lorenzo Vecchietta, specially commissioned by Rossellino, to enrich the primarily Florentine church.

At the time the Duomo was built, workers had to dig 108 feet into the steep clay slope to find ground solid enough for a foundation; and even then, there were fissures and sulfurous fumes to contend with. Ten years after the Duomo was finished, the foundation already showed signs of shifting. The building was gravely damaged by earthquakes in 1545 and again in this century. Although it has been extensively restored in the last few decades, new cracks and other evidence of slippage have continued to appear, and parts of the building have a decidedly dramatic tilt.

Next to the Cathedral is the simple Renaissance Palazzo dei Canonici, now a museum, where an extraordinary papal cope, densely embroidered with scenes from the lives of the saints, is the most notable treasure, and opposite the Duomo, at the beginning of the Corso Rossellino, is the Palazzo Ammanati. Next door is the Palazzo Comunale, with an asymmetrical façade, open loggia, and soaring red brick campanile. Pius completed the piazza by rebuilding palazzi for cardinals whom he persuaded to leave Rome to take up residence with him in Pienza. Among them was Cardinal Rodrigo Borgia, later Pope Alexander VI,

It would be difficult to find cleaner fields anywhere, one cannot see the smallest clod of earth; the soil is as clean as if it had been sifted.

GOETHE
Travels in Italy

who was father to both Lucrezia Borgia and the infamous Cesare. During his time in Pienza, he lived in the austere Bishop's Palace, which had been the town hall before Rossellino remodeled it to fit the elegant harmony of the piazza. The architecture of the entire square combines the red of weathered brick with the white, gold, and soft gray of the travertine and other stones. The buildings themselves are set on the neat herringbone pattern of the square within its travertine grid, and their deep cornices, arches, and pilasters give a classical unity to the whole.

During the three years of building there were rumors that Rossellino was spending far more than the eighteen thousand ducats specified in his estimate. When the Pope called him in after inspecting the work, he said, "You did well, Bernardo, in lying to us about the expense involved in the work. If you had told the truth, you could never have induced us to spend so much money"—the final amount exceeded fifty thousand ducats—"neither this splendid palace nor this church, the finest in all Italy, would now be standing." And he not only ordered the bill to be paid in full, but also gave the architect an extra hundred ducats, a scarlet robe, and a further commission.

When the Pope died in 1464, the work he had begun essentially stopped. Pienza had a brief resurgence when it was used by the Republican exiles of Siena against the Medici Duke Cosimo I in 1555. Even today its rigorous intellectual plan makes it a tiny utopian city that is a stunning evocation of the Renaissance. The surrounding area was deserted by farmers after World War II, when massive numbers of peasants chose to abandon the countryside. It has since been given new life by Sardinian shepherds, who graze their flocks on the slopes above the Val d'Orcia and thus add to the production of the straw-colored sweet pecorino cheese that can be found in the stores along the Corso Rossellino. Leading off this main artery, tiny thoroughfares open into narrow courtyards where old women look out of windows hung with spotless laundry, or make their way along vine-shaded passageways.

Piazza Pio II, Pienza

Palazzo Pretorio, Volterra

Volterra

High on a steep mountainside in a geography of rock and stone, Volterra towers above hills of naked earth, a monochromatic city compelling awe, not because it is higher than any other—at 1,800 feet it is not—but because its stony towers and monumental walls carve hard edges above a dry landscape. Once a proud stronghold and one of the largest cities in Etruria, it sits alone in a somber, undulating landscape, frozen waves in a gray sea, dominating two steep valleys halfway between Siena and the Tyrrhenian Sea, where the land has already turned raw on its way to the Maremma. Olive and vine are almost strangers here. Edith Wharton in *Italian Backgrounds* described the countryside as "a sea of hills" and Volterra "a scaly monster floating on a wave, its savage spine bristling with . . . walls and towers." And if Volterra today is awesome, imagine what it must have been when its massive walls rose forty feet, were thirteen feet thick, and enclosed almost five miles of densely built city. Then all the palaces, temples, and towers filled the entire space within walls so vast that Thomas B. Macaulay, the poet and historian who was also an acclaimed statesman, described them as

The houses on each side were divided only a pace or two, and communicated with one another, here and there, by arched passages. They looked very ancient, and may have been inhabited by Etruscan princes, judging from the massiveness of some of the foundation stones.

NATHANIEL HAWTHORNE
French and Italian Notebooks

Piled by the hands of giants
For godlike kings of old.

At its summit an enormous fortress with sturdy circular dungeons and stubby towers casts a psychological shadow—it has long been a penitentiary—and at the city's edge steep, jagged cliffs called the Balze are slowly disintegrating, leaving a gargantuan hole that consumes whatever lies in its path. These gigantic flawed cliffs, yellow sandstone giving way to gray clay at lower levels, collect the water that falls on Volterra and erodes from below, causing the upper layers to collapse, dragging buildings, walls, and earth in after them. To D. H. Lawrence, whose fascination with Etruscan civilization brought him to Volterra, the Balze were "weird yawning gulfs, like vast quarries. The swallows, turning their blue backs, skim away from the ancient lips and over the really dizzy heights, in the yellow light of evening, catching the upward gusts of wind, then flickering aside like lost fragments of life, truly frightening above those ghostly hollows." A nearby tall medieval church on its carpet of grass, isolated now, has been abandoned to certain doom as the perpetual landslide slowly advances toward it, ready to swallow up one more piece of the past. Etruscan necropoli, early Christian churches, a medieval monastery, houses, and a piece of ancient wall are already buried deep in the earth, layers of city no longer visible at the base of the cliffs. At sunset, when the light turns golden and irradiates this huge abyss and the wind swirls menacingly in its gray depths, it exerts a powerful attraction. It is said that snakes rise upward, unsettled perhaps by the spectral landscape, and that suicides are unable to resist its primal hum.

From its ashen setting, where it sits, according to D. H. Lawrence in *Etruscan Places*, "right in the wind and as cold as any alp," the city looks grim and menacing, but inside its massive walls a giant medieval beauty comes to life in severe palazzi, bold tower houses, and beautiful sloping piazze. Guido Piovene, in *Viaggio in Italia,* calls it "the hardest, most secret, and closed city of Tuscany," and its rough stony beauty certainly has none of the gentle romantic charm of other hill towns set in enchanted Tuscan farmland. Even the Piazza dei Priori, one of the most beautiful squares in Italy, hides behind the stone wall it presents to the street, refusing to offer more than a hint of the austere beauty inside.

The thirteenth century was Volterra's golden age, but beneath the medieval appearance of its buildings and piazze its roots sink deep in human history. Tombs and artifacts of Neolithic settlements precede the ninth through seventh centuries B.C. when it was the center of Villanovan culture, and then became Velathri, one of the largest and most powerful cities in all of Etruria. Fragments of massive fortifications, gigantic uncemented sandstone blocks piled one atop the other, still range far behind the diminished modern city, which has shrunk dramatically to a mere third of its original size.

Chunks of these walls, which Stendhal called "Cyclopean," the "objects of my journey," stretch beneath the fortress on the hill, at the desolate area where the land drops steeply away near the Church of Santa Chiara, and at the Porta all'Arco, the double Etruscan gateway, while pale hints of the city's acropolis are visible in rough remaining fragments near the summit of the hill.

Volterra was one of the last cities to capitulate to Roman aggressiveness. It maintained its economic prosperity and sent Scipio grain, wood, and fittings for the ships of his fleet, but sided with Marius in the civil war between him and Sulla and withstood a two-year siege. Reprisals were swift, and the city was saved from loss of citizenship only by

Cicero's eloquent arguments in its behalf. Even though the city held out against Rome, Volterra was the recipient of baths, temples, and a reservoir, but the Roman theater, preserved for years beneath a landslide of earth, remains the city's most impressive classical monument. Fluted columns with leafy capitals rise within the arc of its semicircular stage, which is set on a shady site for protection from the heat of the summer sun.

A city long intimate with Christianity—St. Linus, St. Peter's successor and the Church's second Pope, came from Volterra, as did three of his successors— Volterra had a diocese as early as Constantine's edict legitimizing the Christian religion. When the empire fell, the city was besieged by Goths and ruled by Lombards and Franks before the warrior bishops in the eleventh century got a grim grip on the city and on the salt and mineral wealth that were the foundation of its prosperity. Forcing the nobles in the nearby countryside to move within its walls, Volterra first rejected the ruling bishop-counts—one was stabbed near the doors of the Duomo in 1270—to become an independent city-state, was Guelph and Ghibelline by turns with all the accompanying turmoil, and then overthrew its ruling signorial family, while keeping up constant battles with San Gimignano, Pisa, Siena, and especially Florence, where expansionist drives were finally successful in subduing the contentious commune. Even so, Volterra staged two rebellions, the first over the nearby alum mines, which led to Florence's sacking the city in 1472, and the second in 1530, when it lost its independence to Florence in a devastating house-to-house battle.

The Piazza dei Priori in the heart of the city remains a truly medieval space that seems essentially unchanged by the passage of seven hundred years. Its high, dark palaces are reserved and secretive, their façades narrowly pierced with windows in broad expanses of stone. The windows themselves are few, and the general severity of their faces masks whatever goes on inside. Attenuated arched doorways, great highground arcades, and the vertical thrust of towers makes the buildings seem extravagantly tall as they crowd tightly at the irregular edges, and their cumulative statement is one of power and hooded strength. In rain and fog, as the wind whips around, the piazza, like the city itself, is monochromatic, grim even, the color of iron; but let the sun shine, warming the stone and creating shadows within the deeply incised window frames, and it has a crisp, austere beauty about it. The light seems to trigger a response deep within the stone, which glows from inside and gives the color back to the world in a tawny ocher tone. There are

We wander on, a little dismally, looking at the stony stoniness of the medieval town. Perhaps on a warm sunny day it might be pleasant, when the shadow was attractive and a breeze welcome. But on a cold, grey windy afternoon of April, Sunday, always especially dismal, with all the people in the streets, bored and uneasy, and the stone buildings peculiarly sombre and hard and resistant, it is no fun. I don't care about the bleak but truly medieval piazza; I don't care if the Palazzo Pubblico has all sorts of amusing coats of arms on it: I don't care about the cold cathedral, though it is rather nice really, with a glow of dusky candles and a smell of Sunday incense: I am disappointed in the wooden sculpture of the taking down of Jesus, and the bas reliefs don't interest me. In short, I am hard to please!

D. H. LAWRENCE
Etruscan Places

buildings of different eras, Renaissance palazzi and later reconstructions, but there is no disharmony or dissonance because they are all made of the same local stones, *panchina,* quarried from nearby hills.

On one side stands the Palazzo Pretorio, a collection of thirteenth-century buildings that rise over enormous ground arches. The rhythms of its few windows are full of single beats and double mullions and arches in a careful, slow cadence. It is anchored by a merloned tower that carries at its top the abstract form of a winsome boar, who gives it the name *porcellino,* "little pig's tower." Boars have roamed the Tuscan hills for centuries and hunting them was very popular sport, but this one, carved of stone and weathered by time, stares fixedly at the dense five-sided tower that rises directly across the square out of the center of the Palazzo dei Priori. The oldest remaining government palace in Tuscany, it is as much fortress as town hall, expressing the power of the commune at its peak. A loggia once softened its sharp lines, but the Florentines destroyed it when they conquered the city and left instead two marble lions, purely political animals, and the sprinkling of glazed terra-cotta and marble coats of arms of its commissioners that grace its lowest level. Five mullioned windows give the slightest syncopation to a sober façade that was the theatrical set for many of the city's bloodiest dramas. It was backdrop for the decapitation of a traitorous ruler who sold the city to Pisa for thirty-two thousand florins, and it later watched the body of Guido Landini sail into the piazza from an upper window, his reward for trying to keep the city free of Florentine domination. Now the only drama lies in the *Annunciations* and *Crucifixions* in the upstairs municipal Gallery, where Taddeo di Bartolo's Sienese figures keep company with Florentine compositions by Ghirlandaio; by Rosso Fiorentino, whose *Deposition* was originally an altarpiece; and by Luca Signorelli, whose *Annunciation* shows God and his angels clustered within a Blakean cloud.

A brief glimpse of black and white bands and the startling introduction of pattern from the neighboring Duomo are the single note of contrast in the stony piazza. Pigeons scutter along the hard pavement and feed on scraps from the markets that are tucked under open arcades. Glossy chestnuts, artichokes, frilly cabbages, and pink and white cranberry beans are piled high on boxes and fussed over by black-aproned women, while old men, deep in the back, bend twigs to form the ubiquitous soft brooms that sweep clean all these medieval streets. The Bishop's Palace, once the public granary, holds sacred art and the remains of churches

swallowed by the Balze, while shops, a restaurant, the post office, and a bank are tucked into the other palazzi, splashes of modern life that scarcely touch the austerity of these buildings.

In the adjacent square the Duomo, Baptistery, and hospital are grouped with serenity. Stripes of green and white marble cover the face of the octagonal Baptistery, which is said to have risen over the ruins of a pagan temple, and inside, only an altar and two fonts—one an old Etruscan cippus, the other by Sansovino—furnish the bare and simple interior space.

The Romanesque Duomo facing it was first built in the twelfth century, then rebuilt in Pisan form, giving a more refined and urban façade to its original rough Romanesque simplicity. It is animated with alternating black and white marble stripes, a marble portal, a lunette inset with geometrical mosaics, graceful small loggias, and a splendid series of capitals and reliefs on the parapet. The interior, all coffered ceiling, pink columns, satins and brocades and baroque flounces, speaks with the voice of later, more extravagant centuries. Here and there, among mannerist altarpieces, are a lyrical Gozzoli fresco that is background to a later crèche, a polychrome *Madonna and Child* that some attribute to Jacopo della Quercia, a carved Romanesque marble pulpit with scenes that include a Last Supper with ominous snakes and monsters beneath the ill-fated table, and special angel candlesticks by Mino da Fiesole.

Beyond the Duomo, down streets that run to the walls, are dozens of alabaster workshops, all of them blanketed in chalky white dust. Ghostly faces, half hidden by the floury white powder that covers every surface, bend over lathes and wheels with intense concentration, cutting and shaving this soft translucent piece of earth from nearby quarries and turning it into the ashtrays, animal figures, and vases that appear in every shop in town. The artisans work as deftly with their tools as their Etruscan ancestors must have when they carved the burial urns that held their cremated ashes, and formed the heads on the huge double gateway of the Porta all'Arco. Thirty feet deep and dark as a tunnel, the bold gate in the medieval wall was originally Etruscan, but all that is left of it now are the massive jambs that make miniatures of the medieval blocks that surround it, and the three enigmatic, featureless faces staring out from the imposing masonry. "It is much the finest piece of real Etruscan architecture I have seen," Roger Fry wrote to Robert Bridges. In fact, the interior of the vault was restored by the Romans and much of the face of the wall was medieval. Fry noticed the same arch on a funerary urn in the museum, with the same figures of dark heads so eroded and worn that no one knows whether they represent enemies conquered in battle or Etruscan deities.

From the ancient gate, medieval grafted onto Etruscan, the street climbs to the center of the city that Gabriele D'Annunzio called "the city of wind and sandstone" in the novel that he set here, *Forse che Sì, Forse che No*. Streets run downhill from the great piazza into a section with towers, tower houses, and an overpass with a house in its center that, like a great arch, makes a daring midair leap, connecting two buildings on either side of the street. Once-fierce tower houses, monuments to ferocity with high vista lookouts, fit tightly next to Renaissance palazzi with rough ashlar bases and low, small windows, sometimes covered with a metal grillwork for protection, that were created especially for children. Here and there a bakery or pharmacy inhabits the first level of some of the dizzily tall buildings, but there is almost no room for the sun to slide down these narrow streets. The pigeons of Volterra nest in openings and on weathered ledges of medieval houses with elegant Gothic arches. Below them, cats slink along toward the shopping street that lies behind the piazza, brush past a solemn Renaissance palazzo by Ammanati that has been turned into a movie theater, next to the intimate piazza dominated by a severe twelfth-century tower. The street carves an uphill path and thickens into a leafy piazza, one of the few spots of green in a severe stony city.

Nearby stands the Etruscan Museum, with one of the greatest Etruscan art collections in Italy, most of its pieces collected by Monsignor Guarnacci, who donated them to the city along with his library of thirty thousand volumes. Every piece of work comes from within the commune of Volterra itself, "the accumulated sepulchral spoil of a century and a half," noted the great scholar George Dennis in his *Cities and Cemeteries of Etruria*. In *Italian Hours* Henry James thought it "a rich and perfectly arrayed museum, an unsurpassed exhibition of monumental treasure from Etruscan tombs, funeral urns mostly, reliquaries of an infinite power to move and charm us still."

These urns are a remarkable picture of everyday life in Etruria, of its religious beliefs, customs, and feelings about death.

D. H. Lawrence was fascinated by the rooms upon rooms of miniature sarcophagi containing the ashes of the dead and wrote in *Etruscan Places* that he "got more

real pleasure out of these Volterrean ash-chests than out of—I had almost said the Parthenon frieze." To him they were like an open book pulsing with life and evoking the vitality of a sensuous and artistic people gone from the earth now for more than two thousand years. On the lid of each is a startlingly vivid and realistic portrait of the deceased, joined to a peculiarly underscaled body, which probably indicates that the chests were mass-produced but the heads made during the lifetime of the subject. On the sides of the boxes are numerous scenes from mythology and contemporary Etruscan life. There are fantastic and ferocious animals, griffins fighting amazons, demons, sea dragons, serpents, Medusas, and devils, symbols of the powers of the inner world, "creatures of the elements," says Lawrence, "which carry men away into death, over the border between the elements." Many scenes come from the Trojan cycle, from myths of Ulysses, from Oedipus and Thebes—almost all carved of alabaster from the local quarries—classic subjects that are "fables," a story used "as a peg upon which the native Volterrean hung his fancy as the Elizabethan used Greek stories for their poems."

In the silent rooms, these ghosts of the past—well-fed men and elegantly dressed matrons, young girls and noblemen—enact scenes from everyday life. Men swim and enjoy themselves at horse races, boar hunts, and gladiatorial events; there are triumphal processions, horrendous animal and human sacrifices, and girls quietly going about their schooling. Some urns emphasize the sensual side of life, with scenes of men and women lying on couches and enjoying banquets, for there is no question that the Etruscans celebrated life with passion even while the shadow of death lay always at their backs. It is in their preoccupation with death and in the numerous scenes depicting their personal feelings about the fleeting nature of life that these urns are most touching. Tender scenes of impending death, of husband and wife embracing for the last time, a brother setting off on his final journey being stopped briefly by a younger sister who tries to prevent the horse leaving, a distraught wife watching her husband driven beyond the boundaries of this world into the next, a grieving family collecting around the bed of a dying mother—these are eloquent expressions of deeply felt emotions. Lawrence was particularly fascinated by the scenes of leave-taking, journeys in covered wagons drawn by horses, in which a man or woman or entire family moves slowly down a road. "This is surely the journey of the soul," perhaps even the funeral procession, "but the memory in the scene seems much deeper than that." An exceptional and famous urn cover shows a husband and wife, she

We walk up the hill and out of the Florence gate, into the shelter under the walls of the huge medieval castle which is now a State prison. There is a promenade below the ponderous walls, and a scrap of sun, and shelter from the biting wind. A few citizens are promenading even now. And beyond, the bare green country rises up in waves and sharp points, but it is like looking at the choppy sea from the prow of a tall ship; here in Volterra, we ride above it all.

D. H. LAWRENCE
Etruscan Places

Poppy field

reclining and looking with a piercing, expressive glance into his eyes.

From the museum it is but a short walk up the hill to the huge medieval fortress, a prison built by the Duke of Athens in 1343 to suppress unhappy citizens of Volterra and enlarged by Lorenzo de' Medici, who added the huge round tower known as the Maschio and sunless circular dungeons. Its first prisoners were the survivors of the Pazzi conspiracy that killed Lorenzo's brother, and since 1816 the fortress has been a penitentiary for the most hardened criminals. Beneath its towering walls lies a stretch of grassy public park where citizens walk, sheltered from the powerful wind. "And beyond," says Lawrence, "the bare green country rises up in waves and sharp points, but it is like looking at the choppy sea from the prow of a tall shop; here in Volterra, we ride above it all." The view from this hill stretches as far as the blue waters of the Mediterranean, north to the jagged white marble mountains of Carrara, and south over the Metalliferous Hills, with their quarries of alum, salt, and alabaster, to the edges of Elba, while inland Volterra looks over the cinnamon tiles of roof shelving to the walls and to the rich geometry of fertile Tuscan land. The French painter Corot went to Volterra in 1834 in search of fresh visual stimulation, called it "a magnificent bit of country," and stayed a month. He painted several landscapes and a picture of the citadel with the blazing summer sun highlighting the strong clearcut forms of distant buildings of the city. Henry James, too, remembered with pleasure "the vast rake of the view," for the sharp division between medieval city and wild landscape gives Volterra an incomparable identity. It remains a fortress city on a fantastic hilltop, hard edges commanding a harsh landscape, city of the Middle Ages grafted onto the Etruscan, presided over by the dead spirits of Etruria and the dense urban beauty at its heart.

Traffic mirror

Cortona

Secluded on a high spur of Monte Egidio, Cortona is so ancient that it is called "the mother of Troy and the grandmother of Rome." According to Vergil, it was from here that Dardanus went off to found the Trojan race, long before Aeneas left Troy to become the founder of Rome. The Umbrians had occupied the hillside before the Etruscans made Cortona one of their principal cities, draining the Chiana Valley at its foot and fortifying the town with enormous blocks of sandstone quarried from its mountain. Etruscan tombs, including one called the Tomb of Pythagoras—although the Greek philosopher lived not here but in the town of Crotone in what is now Calabria—have been found hidden among the cypress groves in the soft soil at the foot of the town.

Early in the morning, as the thick fog begins to burn off, leaving fingers of white stretching up toward the town, the great cupola of Madonna del Calcinaio rises above the valley, where small islands of trees appear to float in a misty white sea. Two thousand years ago this same promontory looked down as far as Lake Trasimeno and the ambush engineered by Hannibal in his victory over Flaminius and his Roman Legions. The citizens of Cortona were used to the low fogs of the valley, but the panicky Roman soldiers, trapped by the unfamiliar cloud cover and set upon by troops hiding on the heights, were cut down on the spot; those who ran in confusion plunged into the lake and drowned.

The city is perched at the very top of this hill, and its windswept summit, where a long stretch of Etruscan wall still remains, is a military fortress built by the Medici, which has recently been converted into a museum. Just below the isolated ridge stands the Church of Santa Margherita, and descending from the cypresses below it, steeply staired streets offer knife-thin slices of view or drop suddenly into tiny interior courtyards. At the center of the city, beyond the dark falls of stairs and the steep slope of streets, is the two-level Piazza della Repubblica, where the sun washes over the austere medieval and Renaissance façades.

The piazza is the heart of the densely built city. Here people stop to talk, to nod at the priest as he passes, or to finger the candlesticks in a little antique shop while keeping an eye on the postman as he walks his Vespa down the steep slant of the square. House-wives can buy fish on cool beds of ice in the stone arcade of the loggia near the Passerini House, the thirteenth-century stone tower that was once the Palazzo dei Capitani del Popolo and that still dominates the upper level. Across from it rises the town hall with a staircase that absorbs almost the entire lower half of the façade in its ceremonial climb to the central door. The building dates from the thirteenth century, but the steps, like the chunky merloned tower and a wing pierced by an arched opening for traffic, were added three hundred years later. From the upper piazza the street drops sharply, and at midday there is a brief flurry of activity as clumps of schoolboys pass by on their way home for lunch, shopkeepers lock their doors on the single level street in town, and businessmen cross to the elegant restaurant set within a brick-vaulted building nearby.

The asymmetrical Piazza Signorelli, named for the city's most famous citizen, funnels off to one side of the town hall. Luca Signorelli was born here in 1441, and the museums and churches are full of his paintings. Many have a muscularity and powerful line that combine the classical tradition of his teacher, Piero della Francesca, with the Tuscans' close attention to anatomy. Signorelli painted for his patron Lorenzo de' Medici and was called upon to complete the cycle of frescoes on the walls of the Sistine Chapel, but most of the work he did in Corona came near the end of his life. A two-sided altarpiece hangs in that little low-walled stone church of San Nicolò with its cypress-lined courtyards, and a dramatic *Deposition* is one of the nine works that hang in the Diocesan Museum. Signorelli's paintings seem to take some of their essential spirit from the city and landscape of Cortona itself. There is a precision to the anatomy of Cortona that recalls Signorelli's figures in their shading, their square muscular forms, their cool and slightly metallic edge. They appear to have been touched by the same bracing air that passes over the dark stones of the city's austere, virile palaces with their wrought-iron details.

At one corner of the Piazza Signorelli stands the Palazzo Pretorio, a magnificent building that once housed the ruling Casali family and is now the Etruscan Museum. It was founded in the eighteenth century when the city was the center of Etruscomania, and serious archeological research in the area led to the discovery of thousands of amulets, vases, and bronzes inside tombs, revealing the remarkable culture that once flourished in the surrounding countryside. Those

artifacts that remain include attenuated bronzes of women and warriors, numerous animals, and a celebrated bronze lamp that is considered one of the most extraordinary surviving examples of Etruscan workmanship. The sixteen-wick lamp, which must once have cast its light from the ceiling of a tomb, has bands of priapic satyrs and winged sirens, dolphins sporting in sea waves, and wild beasts circling around the face of a Gorgon that bristles with hideous rage and primitive energy. The rest of the museum's collection includes Renaissance paintings and medals by Antonio Pisanello, along with works by Gino Severini, Cortona's most famous modern painter, and a library of thirty thousand volumes.

A short distance below stands the Cathedral, and across from it, in the Piazza del Duomo, is the Diocesan Museum. Formerly the Chiesa del Gesù, constructed with a baptistery above and an oratory below, it now houses an extraordinary collection of Tuscan paintings, including works by Duccio and Pietro Lorenzetti of the fourteenth century and by Sassetta and Signorelli from the fifteenth and early sixteenth, as well as an exceptionally moving *Annunciation* by Fra Angelico. In it, in a moment of stillness and tenderness, the angel comes to Mary in the loggia, where she reads within a little garden, and spills the golden words of his announcement. The brilliant red of the angel's dress with its bands of golden embroidery, the finely beaten gold of his wings, the rich blue of Mary's cape, and the white columns and flowers studding the lawn have a luminosity whose loveliness recalls Seán O'Faoláin's description of Fra Angelico's paintings as being "like music transformed into colour." Its predella includes scenes depicting identifiable neighboring towns, for Fra Angelico lived at a monastery in Cortona for ten years.

Below the Duomo stretches the Via del Gesù, a row of medieval houses jutting out on wooden corbels, while nearby palazzi are stamped with the vigor of the rusticated stones of the Renaissance.

The streets of Cortona radiate outward toward the gates in the huge stone walls that encircle it. Dignity and severity cling to the cool gray-brown stones of its palazzi. Some have high "doors of the dead" originally opened only in case of a death in the family to transport the casket and then bricked up, or powerful arches, carved grills, and rings to hold torches, while the muscular forms of others are offset by the delicacy of a fan window whose wrought iron is worked like fine lace. Narrow streets become stairways scaling the hill, and rooftops extend over the curving stone walls of houses to communicate across the narrow openings between them, a spatial conversation punctuated by a brisk flap of laundry or a single tree reaching for the sun.

From the great Porta Colonia, north of the cathedral, that opens from the city wall with its Etruscan base and medieval body, there are views over a countryside that still seems to have come from a Renaissance painting, with cypress-studded hillsides crowned with umbrella pines, terraced olive groves divided by dry stone walls, streams winding among the farms, and clusters of red-tiled houses. Here and there are haystacks—some shaped like houses, and others with the conical form once visible across both Umbria and Tuscany.

At the top of the city, past weathered stone houses with tufts of green growing in their ancient crevices and geraniums flowering on their balconies, past the rough façade of San Francesco, which is the second earliest Franciscan church of Italy, and past the private gardens at the edge of the city lies the cobbled piazza of the Church of Santa Margherita. The church was originally built in the thirteenth century but was reconstructed in the nineteenth, and now the Gothic tomb of the saint is the only monument of any interest. St. Margherita is the patron saint of Cortona. She grew up in a nearby village very much neglected and mistreated, and when she fell in love with a young man from Montepulciano, she ran away and lived with him happily for nine years, during which she bore him a son. When she found him murdered one day, she was convinced that his death was a punishment for her sin, and she resolved to dedicate herself to a life of repentance through religion. A voice told her to go to the Franciscans of Cortona, and there she embarked on a lifelong ascetic existence, embracing religion with the same intensity that she had once embraced her lover. She remained in Cortona for the rest of her life, caring for the poor and the sick and becoming so important to the people of the city that they built a church to her four hundred years before she was officially canonized.

The elegant Renaissance Church of Santa Maria del Calcinaio sits outside the city gates in a countryside sprinkled with farmhouses, just beyond the groves of olives that edge the road winding up to the city. It rises where once a leather tannery stood and owed its name to a lime burner in the pit where leather skins were treated who found the miraculous image of the Virgin that led to the construction of the church. Its soaring interior, built to house the multitudes of pilgrims who came to worship, is one harmonious light-filled space

that opens beneath an octagonal dome. The clean geometry and elegant clarity of the architecture reflect the Sienese sensibility of its architect, Francesco di Giorgio Martini, as he was influenced by the classicism of Alberti and Brunelleschi and by the luminous example of the Ducal Palace at Urbino.

Cortona was so far from the main routes of travel that many visitors were unaware of its presence. Thomas B. Macaulay was an exception. In his poem "Horatius" he described the clans of Etruria marching down from their hilltops to join Lars Porsena in his campaign to reinstate the exiled Tarquin king of Rome

. . . where Cortona lifts to heaven
Her diadem of towers.

Few of those towers remain today, although the dramatic merloned shaft of Il Palazzone on the shoulder of Cortona's hill rises over a complex of buildings commissioned by Silvio, Cardinal Passerini, where, according to some sources, Signorelli fell to his death from a scaffold while he was painting a fresco in the chapel.

When Henry James accidentally arrived at Cortona on the feast day of Santa Margherita, he was annoyed because it meant that the museum was closed and the churches extremely crowded. His pique subsided as he entered into the spirit of the day and climbed the winding hill up to the Church of Santa Margherita, where he settled himself, alternatively reading and marveling at the view. Now many foreign writers live in Cortona and while bells still ring out as they did when James was there and the squares still fill up on *festa* days, "grim-visaged Cortona, that most sturdily ancient of all Italian towns," as he described it, remains as silent and somber on its hillside as it was in his day, its austere stone palaces and steep runs of stairs virtually unchanged since the Renaissance.

Mantel detail

Set on a gently elongated slope that is less elevated—and thus less protected—than the position of most others, Arezzo is an anomaly among hill towns, one that is, as Hawthorne observed more than a century ago, "much more modern and less picturesque." It stands just above the meeting place of three fertile Tuscan valleys, near where the Arno veers north toward Florence. Fragments of several circuits of wall describe its perimeters in Etruscan, Roman, and medieval times; but now the city has spilled beyond the wide boulevard that was the boundary of its medieval core. That core spans its hill like a great bishop's cope, with streets fanning downward and intersecting others that carve concentric rings about the slope. The ocher and honey colors of the buildings have a cool, gritty edge, in keeping with Arezzo's aggressive energy and bustle.

The most famous of the Etruscan relics found at Arezzo—the *Chimera,* and the bronze *Minerva* that was restored by Benvenuto Cellini in the sixteenth century—have been removed to the Archaeological Museum in Florence, but Arezzo's own Museo Archeologico contains many treasures, among them a collection of the Aretine vases that were acclaimed by Vergil and Pliny. Decorated with incised patterns portraying banquets, sacrificial ceremonies, and mythological figures, this clay pottery is the deep red color of coral. It was first made in Arezzo in the time of Augustus, and for two hundred years was used throughout the entire Roman world. The building that houses the museum was originally an Olivetan monastery that had itself incorporated stones and arches from the Roman amphitheater, which remains the best-preserved Roman monument and sits in a grassy plot in the lower town.

Although it sat astride the Via Cassia, Arezzo's military and economic importance in Roman times did not save it from decline as the great empire waned, or from Gothic invasions in the days of Totila—or, indeed, from a Saracen attack in the late ninth century. But by the eleventh century, under the guidance of a series of pugnacious warrior bishops, Arezzo had begun to expand and once again had an intense civil life. As one of Tuscany's earliest free communes, it flexed its muscles in the direction of neighboring small towns and petty nobles, forcing the nobles to move within its walls for their own protection—all the while warring with nearby Florence, Cortona, and Perugia, and even with far-off Siena. Originally Guelph, Arezzo later changed alliances and became the only Ghibelline city in the region of eastern Tuscany. After the ruling Guelphs of Florence won decisively at the Battle of Campaldino, they sent the Ghibellines of Arezzo into exile in 1289, after first having burned their houses. Dante was one of those who fought against Arezzo on the plain under the castle of Poppi; though he later described the Aretines as "snarling dogs, more fierce than formidable," he also admitted to having been greatly frightened during the battle.

Continual war and political upheaval did not interfere with the city's growth, and Arezzo prospered under the feudal rule of its bishops. The most powerful of these was Guido Tarlati, who fortified the town with new walls, restored the Palazzo Comunale and other civic buildings, and encouraged Sienese and Florentine painters to enhance their interiors. After his death in 1327, Arezzo's importance began to wane. In 1337 his brothers sold its allegiance to Florence, and although for a brief period it recovered its liberty, Arezzo was consigned to permanent domination in 1384 when a mercenary received forty thousand gold coins for delivering it into the hands of the Florentines.

From the beginning, Arezzo was famous for its illustrious citizens. Michelangelo, born in nearby Caprese, told Vasari, "If I have any good in my brain, it comes from being born in the pure air of your country of Arezzo." Long before, it had been the city of Maecenas, friend of the emperor Augustus and patron of Horace and Vergil. It was also the birthplace of the poet Petrarch; of the playwright and satirist Pietro Aretino; and of Guido Giorgio Vasari, the sixteenth-century architect and painter who became the first art historian and is now chiefly remembered for his gossipy *Lives of the Most Eminent Architects, Painters, and Sculptors,* with stories and descriptions that often came from personal acquaintance with the artists. Andrea Sansovino lived and worked here, and Piero della Francesca, one of the greatest of Renaissance painters, was born in nearby Sansepolcro. Aldous Huxley, who went to Arezzo to see

Grey mists of olive branches, warm smoking earth, creamy flanks of oxen, brown limbs and dark eyes of men.

JOHN ADDINGTON SYMONDS
Sketches of Travel in Greece and Rome

his famous frescoes, was not enchanted. "Now Arezzo is a boring sort of town," he wrote in *Along the Road,* "and so ungrateful to its distinguished sons that there is no monument within its walls to the divine Aretino. I deplore Arezzo, nevertheless, you must go to see Piero's most considerable works."

From outside, the severe unfinished stone and brick façade of the Church of San Francesco gives no hint of these works—the major cycle of frescoes by Piero della Francesca. Using a soft palette of hues found in the Tuscan countryside, he painted *The Legend of the True Cross* from its origins at the death of Adam— from whose grave a shoot of the Tree of Knowledge will provide the wood of the Cross—through King Solomon and two rival emperors, down to the Byzantine emperor who triumphantly returns the Cross to Jerusalem at the climax of its long history. The story was familiar to an enormous audience as part of the *Golden Legend of the Saints,* a book known throughout all of Europe in the Middle Ages.

Piero had been a student of Domenico Veneziano—from whom, as Bernard Berenson tells us, he learned to depict human character—and of Paolo Uccello, whose study of the principles of perspective influenced these frescoes, especially the battle scene with its overlapping figures of soldiers and horses. Light pervades the entire series; it illuminates the serene human forms and in one particular composition mysteriously bathes the great birdlike angel bringing a vision of the True Cross to the sleeping Emperor Constantine. Although water damage has obliterated some details, it is still easy to see the beautiful classical architecture, the timeless serenity and stillness of the human forms, and the pewtery reflections from the armor of the horses, as they come to us across the centuries.

Though many medieval churches and towered houses remain, their campaniles adorned with Guelph and Ghibelline crenellations, only one of its Romanesque monuments escaped the destruction of Cosimo I, who leveled the oldest part of the city to replace its walls and rebuild his fortress. He spared the Pieve of Santa Maria, which, like so much else in Arezzo, rises upon the shelf of an even older structure, one that was built at the beginning of the eleventh century. The façade of rough sandstone is animated by three tiers of columns, rising one upon the other like the graceful thirteenth-century churches of Pisa and Lucca. Each column is different from every other; some are composed of twisting and curving spirals, some incised with budding flowers or writhing snakes and creeping

Oxen in Tuscan vineyard

vines, some fluted and intricately carved. The capitals are still more varied, while other examples of the stone carver's art appear in charming Lombard vignettes of men working in harmony with nature—workers prune olive trees in February, thresh grain in July, and gather grapes in the sunshine of September.

From this church, built by the commune of Arezzo, a narrow street leads to the Piazza Grande, which opens behind it. This was the original commercial and civic center of Arezzo, and once a year, seven centuries later, it still plays host to the colorful Joust of the Saracen—a spectacle in which horsemen wearing medieval costume ride at full tilt, lances extended, toward the wooden image of an enormous Saracen. One hand of the figure holds a target, the other a rotating spiky mace; and the rider who comes closest to

scoring a direct hit, without being knocked off his horse or whacked on the head, takes home a Golden Lance to his neighborhood quarter.

The Piazza Grande also comes to life one Sunday each month, when it is the scene of a furniture fair to which people come from great distances, hoping to unearth a real Etruscan fragment or a Renaissance treasure from among the assortment of chairs, candlesticks, old coins, chests, and grandfather clocks that are spread out for sale in the marketplace.

On quieter days, it is pleasant to wander about the asymmetrical piazza that slopes from Vasari's gracefully arcaded Renaissance loggia to the medieval houses at its foot. The space is paved with rosy brick in a herringbone pattern, with insets of travertine triangles and circles. Towers and fine old stone buildings climb one steep side, and the other becomes, in effect, a condensed history of architecture—from the hemisphere of the Romanesque apse to an eighteenth-century tribunal, or court of justice—just as the silent gray interior of the Pieve is an encyclopedia of decoration: the lively animal heads forming the capitals are Lombard; the Madonna and Child that tower over three adoring Magi are Byzantine; and the pointed arches of the presbytery that was added to the original Romanesque body of the church are Gothic. The Campanile that towers almost two hundred feet overhead is known as the "bell tower with a hundred windows," for the mullioned openings that pierce it on every side.

Beyond the Palazzo Pretorio, on whose façade are carved the coats of arms of the Florentine commissioners who rule Arezzo, the Corso Italia continues its upward climb to the fortress built by the Medici over an earlier citadel. The walls and ramparts designed by Antonio da Sangallo still remain in place, overlooking red-tiled roofs and towers and the vines and silvery olives that cover the slopes beyond the town. To the north are rolling green hills that range as far as the Apennines. When Henry James visited the "old pacified citadel" in 1873, he pronounced himself enormously pleased with the spot and its view. In *Italian Hours* he wrote, "Beautiful hills surround it, cypresses cast straight shadows at its corners, while in the middle grew a wondrous tangle of wheat and corn, vines and figs, peaches and cabbage, memories and images, anything and everything."

Today, in a densely planted public garden, children play soccer on a shade-dappled playground, and men and women stroll under the umbrella pines, sycamores, and elms that line the walks. It is a short upward walk to the Duomo, which rises above a stairway that serves as a pedestal and makes a ceremony of the act of ascending. The soaring interior space, like that of a northern European Gothic cathedral, is lit by brilliantly colored glass windows, which Vasari

described as "something rained down from heaven for the consolation of man." Their rich colors and forms come from the hand of the Frenchman Guillaume de Marcillat, who fled to Italy to avoid imprisonment for a crime. When Charles Dickens came to Italy with his family, he stopped in Arezzo and went to mass in the Cathedral he later described in *Pictures from Italy* as "where the sun shines in among the clustered pillars through rich stained glass windows, half revealing, half concealing the kneeling figures on the pavement, and striking out paths of light in the long aisles." The tomb of San Donato, the martyred patron saint of Arezzo, combines pinnacles and airy trefoiled turrets of white marble with a mosaic of scenes from his life. Another tomb commemorates the life of Bishop Tarlati, the city's most important warrior lord. Beside this monument is Piero della Francesca's luminous fresco of Mary Magdalen.

During the Renaissance, new religious and civic buildings went up, often directly over earlier oratories and abbeys, to the elegant designs of Bartolomeo della Gatta, Benedetto and Giuliano da Maiano, and Antonio da Sangallo, who originally came to rebuild the city's defenses. The hand of Vasari, which transformed much of Florence, is visible in numerous buildings that he remodeled in the mannerist style, as well as in the paintings that decorate their walls and altars. And the walls of his own house swirl with colossal figures depicting allegorical themes.

For all of its historical layers, the present is very much alive in Arezzo, and where armored knights once clattered over the cobblestones, the footsteps of preoccupied businessmen and the staccato of women's high heels are now to be heard. If Arezzo has little of the romantic charm of the rest of Tuscany, it does have the liveliness, confidence, and economic prosperity of a thriving commercial center, whose streets are full of shops selling the latest fashions to successful young Aretines.

Country hillside

Umbria

Umbria has long been known as the green heart of Italy. It lies deep in the center of the country and is the only region that touches neither the sea nor a foreign frontier, and as a consequence is somewhat withdrawn, a landscape that turns in upon itself. The population of this intimate region numbers a mere eight hundred thousand, most of whom are contained within its low wooded hills and cultivated valleys. More than half of Umbria is steeply mountainous, and almost all of the rest is hilly, with fertile green valleys watered by numerous streams that spill down from the hills. It is shaped by chains of wooded mountains whose broad domes and rounded tops are more regular here than elsewhere in the Apennines; the rugged limestone hills of the east are more steeply compact, while the western slopes drop in longer, more gradual slopes and spurs. The serenity of this rustic region with its profound respect for the human dimension of life may be a reflection of its geography, for, like the human heart it resembles in form, Umbria remains a quiet spiritual center that once harbored the meditative mysticism of St. Francis, who expressed the spirituality of the Italian people.

Between two and five million years ago, the entire western part of Umbria was invaded by the sea, which left behind deposits of clay and yellowish sands and eroded the mountains to produce the undulations we see today. Of the chains of lakes left behind, the only ones of any size now remaining are Corbara, which is fed by the Tiber; tiny Piediluco in the east; and Trasimeno, outside Perugia, the area's most popular resort, whose milky blue waters are pierced by spiky reeds and inhabited by pike, eel, carp, perch, and trout. The Tiber, which winds through the entire length of the region, divides Umbria between east and west. An old Umbrian saying has it that "there would be no Tiber if the Nera did not give it drink," and in fact this famous river, which starts high in the Tuscan Apennines, is more stream than torrent in these early beginnings and has none of the power and size it gains as it approaches Rome. Of the other streams that course among the Umbrian hills—the Chiascio, the Topino, the Tessino, the Paglia, the Clitunno—none ever reaches impressive proportions. The most imposing presence of water is the enormous waterfall of the Marmore, the highest in Italy, which drops 165 meters. Joseph Addison found it more astonishing than the waterworks of Versailles, but today the great falls, which were created by the Romans, are diverted to create

Church interior, Cività di Bagnorégio, near Orvieto

Overgrown garden, villa near Spello

electric power, and are visible only on weekends and holidays.

The Umbrian region as defined under the emperor Augustus had somewhat different boundaries from those of today and extended from the Tiber to the Adriatic. Over the centuries, the Tiber came to be replaced as the region's main thoroughfare by the great Flaminian Way, built by the Romans when they embarked on the unifying of central Italy. Since those times the Via Flaminia has served emperors, popes, dukes, *condottieri* intent on conquest, and pilgrims en route to Rome. The modern Via Flaminia is a later diversion; as state road 3, one of today's *superstrade*, it runs between Terni and Spoleto before arriving at Foligno in the plain, which it then links with Perugia, now the largest city in the region. When the Via Flaminia was first built, it ran from Rome northward through Trevi (then Trebiae), Spello (Hispellum), and Montefalco (then known as Coccurione) and then northeastward to Gualdo Tadino, where Totila was killed, toward the Scheggia Pass, and over the Apennines to the Adriatic.

The cities built during the years of Umbria's

richest flowering remain for the most part very little changed, and their cathedrals and castles preserve the medieval intimacy of the countryside. Some appear to spill down a mountain flank, as at Assisi, Gubbio, and Trevi, or to climb the curve of a hill, as at Spoleto, whereas some in Tuscany sit on the summit of an isolated hill. The contours of the land appear softer and the valleys more open than those in the fractured and densely inhabited Tuscan countryside, where the uplands are dotted with numerous little towns. The best land in Umbria lies in what were once lake basins. Everywhere in the Tiber Valley and in the lowland between Perugia and Spoleto, neatly pruned olives and vines, fruit trees, and elms parade down the slopes toward the plains that are planted with corn, sunflowers, wheat, tobacco, and alfalfa, dotted here and there with conical haystacks.

Dense forests once covered the Umbrian hills, but human beings early began to alter the natural balance of the countryside. When the Romans became a naval power and built an extensive fleet, they clear-cut many of the Apennine mountaintops for wood—a precedent that was to be repeated by the shipbuilders of Pisa,

Genoa, and Venice. They felled numerous trees whose timbers were used for building and for fuel. Many Latin writers document the practice of cutting trees to create meadows for the grazing of cattle and to make room for vineyards, orchards, and wheat fields. Pliny in his *Natural History* traced the cultivation and diffusion of olive trees—Umbrian olive oil remains among the world's finest—and Vergil described the arching tops of beeches, oaks, and pines, and the grassy meadows where sheep and goat fed. As migratory shepherds drove their flocks to pasture, these animals fed on young beeches and chestnuts, nibbling at their leaves, stripping them bare, or eating them away completely. As the small trees disappeared, forests gave way to the open meadows dotted with trees that form the bucolic settings for Umbrian paintings of the Madonna or the lives of the saints. Grazing artificially extended the countryside and reached up the mountainsides, further diminishing the variety of vegetation.

Sheep and goats still graze on the grasses and wild herbs of the hills, and the Chianina cattle from near Perugia and the pigs of the Tiber Valley provide the spit-roasted and grilled meat for which Umbria is famous. The vines on its hillsides are made into the pale golden wines of Orvieto, the lesser-known vintages of the Colli Perugini, and the Colli del Trasimeno, the wines of Montefalco, and the rich Rubescoes and cabernet sauvignons from the vineyards at Torgiano near Perugia. From the wheat come pastas produced on an industrial scale by giant companies such as Buitoni, which has headquarters at Perugia. The famous black truffles of Italy are dug out of the earth around Spoleto and Norcia in the mountainous east.

Today Umbria no longer depends primarily on its agriculture. Many farmers have left the countryside to work in the cities, and the practice of agriculture itself is changing. Until quite recently the main form of land tenure, which dates back to the sixteenth century in Umbria, and in Tuscany as far back as the eleventh, had been the *mezzadria* system of share-cropping, under which a tenant lived in a house provided by the landowner, working the land with tools and animals similarly provided, in return for a small rental and a proportion of the crop. Over the past twenty-five years a straight rental has superseded the *mezzadria*. In parts of Umbria, machines that eliminate the hard work of cultivating the soil have done away with the mixed cultivation of vines, grain, fruit trees, and olives that until recent decades had prevailed here, as in Tuscany, and single-crop agriculture is now taking its place.

While almost eight hundred years have passed since St. Francis began the pilgrimage that took him across the entire Umbrian plain in the thirteenth century, he would undoubtedly still recognize it, for the look of the region has been little changed by the centuries. A panoramic view of it is offered by the little town of Montefalco, reached along a road that winds upward from the Via Flaminia. Often called the "Balcony of Umbria," Montefalco is situated at the heart of the region, and on a clear day it is possible to see as far north as Perugia and almost as far south as Spoleto. In between, the geometric pattern of the cultivated farmland contained in the undulating valleys is punctuated by cypresses, long files of poplars, and the dark green of oaks, by the fields of golden broom in summer and the bright red of springtime poppies.

To the west, in the region once dominated by the Etruscans, there is a change in the landscape, first in the low hill country and then in the plateau where steep, fluted cliffs of tufa rock thrust up like islands above the morning mists. Periodic eruptions by a string of now extinct volcanoes created these pedestals of solidified volcanic ash, and their craters form the basins of the few remaining lakes. The towns of Orvieto, Orte, and Città di Bagnorégio in neighboring Lazio rest on these strange mesas of land as though stranded by a deluge, overlooking green slopes and flatland notable for the fertility of its volcanic soils. The harsh wild country beneath the high Apennine spine to the east is remote and secluded, a retreat from modern life as it was once a shelter for St. Benedict.

From the mountains themselves come the materials that gave the hill towns their individual character: Orvieto's porous, tawny volcanic tufa; Assisi with its soft pink and gray limestone; the harder, more austere gray of Gubbio; the pinks and grays of Spello on a low flank of Monte Subasio. Marble of various colors was brought from farther away to brighten the inner walls and floors of dark palaces, to make forests of interior columns, and to ornament piazze with statues and ceremonial wells.

Some of the smaller towns are among the most picturesque and most ancient. Spello was known as Hispellum in Roman times, when it was an important religious center. Its walls and gates were built by Augustus, who expropriated houses and land in the vicinity to give to his favorite followers. The poet Propertius complained bitterly in one of his verses of the property he lost this way. It was under Constantine the Great, however, that the town reached the height of its importance, when religious celebrations took place in a temple built specifically for such occasions. Despite internal divisions, Spello managed to hold out against

Frederick II, but succumbed to the power of the Popes in 1535, when some of its walls were dismantled. On the feast of Corpus Christi, the town's main piazza, situated halfway up the hill, becomes a carpet of flowers arranged in complex designs depicting religious scenes, for a celebration known as the Infiorata. The chief Roman remnants include the sturdy Porta Consolare and an imposing barrel-vaulted gate from Augustan times known as the Porta Venere for the Temple of Venus that once stood next to it. Farther up the hill, reached through narrow, winding lanes wrapped with the arched overpasses that give the city its particular personality profile, is a belvedere overlooking the grassy ellipse of a Roman amphitheater. Nearby stands a Romanesque church built on the remains of a Roman basilica, whose altar incorporates the top of a sarcophagus. But the chief ornament of the city is the frescoes of Pinturicchio in the Baglioni Chapel of the Church of Santa Maria Maggiore, with their lyrical feeling and richly intricate details of the Umbrian countryside.

The cobbled streets of nearby Trevi are so precipitously steep that the roofs appear to have been stacked one above the other. The city spills down the hillside from the point of its campanile like white lava oozing down a cone of land. The surrounding slopes are once again dense with olive trees that have replaced many killed by the intense cold of the winter of 1956. A thick clump of willows to the south marks the source of the river Clitunno, just above where Spoleto stands guard upon the valley. Celebrated by Vergil and Propertius—who knew it as Clitumnus—and later by Dryden, Byron, and Carducci, its cool, limpid waters were used by the Romans for the ceremonial washing of sacrificial bulls. Pliny the Younger wrote of the popularity of these waters as a tourist attraction at a time when villas lined the river's edge, and their crystalline purity today draws picnickers and visitors by the hundreds to what has remained a relatively unspoiled setting. Nearby stands the Tempietto del Clitunno, a small round church built in the early fifth century over the remains of a pagan temple. Its frescoes, dating from the seventh century, are thought to be the oldest in Umbria. It is one of a handful of early Christian churches still remaining from the period immediately following the declaration of the emperor Constantine permitting Christians to worship openly. In Umbria most of these churches—Sant'Angelo at Perugia and San Salvatore at Spoleto are exceptions—were destroyed during the barbarian invasions.

Even Montefalco, which was once a Roman site, became a battleground for the armies of Pope and Emperor during its days as a free commune of the Middle Ages. It was captured by Frederick Barbarossa and totally sacked by an emissary of his grandson, Frederick II. Until then it was known as Coccurione, but its name was changed between 1249 and 1250, perhaps because, according to an often repeated story, a *falco* (hawk) that appeared was considered a good omen, or perhaps because an imperial hawk remained in the free commune.

Nowadays the quiet of the little town that has been called "a strip of heaven fallen to earth" is interrupted only by the occasional arrival of tourists drawn by the paintings of Benozzo Gozzoli in the Church of San Francesco. These cheerful, sunlit frescoes of the life of the saint who spent his days walking from town to town in this same region show a green landscape of walled towns, the bare summit of Monte Subasio, and the softly shaded valleys that appear to have changed little since they were painted. Berenson described Gozzoli as a "Fra Angelico who had forgotten heaven and became enamored of the earth and its springtime," and his paintings capture the Franciscan acceptance of the natural environment, Umbria as the original garden. The artistic tradition in Umbria, visible in many such paintings in many small hill towns, is devoted almost exclusively to saints and Madonnas set in grassy meadows arched over by a luminous sky. Both Pinturicchio and Perugino capture not only the Umbrian landscape, with towns on the distant hills, but the melting soft light and gentle atmosphere that is particularly Umbrian. Perhaps because of its remoteness from direct routes of communication, Umbria never developed a tradition with the richness of Tuscany. And once the region fell under the shadow of the papacy, evidence of Umbrian vitality in the arts and architecture simply ebbed away. After Signorelli, Perugino, and Pinturicchio, no new masters appeared. The Umbrian drive for self-expression was stifled and allowed to die or driven underground.

The stones of these hill towns speak a language that is a rich blend of dialects. What they share is the way they grew organically in relation to the landscape with intimate narrow streets, runs of stairs, and open piazze creating a pattern as complex as medieval tapestries. Today the very geography that created them has preserved them essentially as they were in medieval and Renaissance times, when, as fortified towns high above the valleys, they were a source of refuge from invading armies. Umbria, set between Florence, Rome, and Ravenna, was the meeting point of various artistic currents. The monasteries that initially encouraged

Detail, door, Duomo, Todi

artistic development were supplanted by the patronage of the Church and, by the twelfth century, the independent communes themselves constructed civic palazzi and ambitious cathedrals that were ornamented by artists whose frescoes and sculpture still remain. The buildings carve a civic identity in stone, and while their populations may be tiny, the towns are celebrations of an urban vitality and represent continuity with the Etruscans who first taught the Romans to live in cities. Today the hill towns are left with the rich heritage of their ambitious pasts and they remain the collective memory of a culture, an unbroken link with history.

Duomo, Perugia

Perugia

I should, perhaps, do the reader a service by telling him just how a week at Perugia may be spent. His first care must be to ignore the very dream of haste, walking everywhere very slowly and very much at random, and to impute an esoteric sense to almost anything his eye may happen to encounter. Almost everything in fact lends itself to the historic, the romantic, the aesthetic fallacy—almost everything has an antique queerness and the richness that ekes out the reduced state; that of a grim and battered old adventuress, the heroine of many shames and scandals, surviving to an extraordinary age and a considerable penury, but with ancient gifts of princes and other forms of the wages of sin to show, and the most beautiful garden of all the world to sit and doze and count her beads and remember.

HENRY JAMES
Italian Hours

The largest and most vigorous of Umbrian hill towns, Perugia sprawls across the ridges of its sandy cliffs and dominates a superb site more than a thousand feet above the Tiber Valley. Today the city reaches far beyond the medieval walls and stern Etruscan gates that once circumscribed it, and sits above the unremitting traffic that winds up the hill, its buildings a flash of stone and red tile roofs hovering restlessly over the plain. It still commands the hilltop like a medieval fortress, but the aggressions and expansionist drives that motivated its nobles and warriors during the Middle Ages and early Renaissance today find expression in commerce and industry. Perugina chocolates, elegant knits, and Buitoni pastas are made here and exported around the world. The violence of the past has been replaced by a more hedonistic spirit and Perugia has become a bustling modern city. The small industrial factories and nondescript apartment buildings that spill down from its old gateways and walls in a jumble make it the rare hill town with sizable noisy and competitive suburbs.

At its center, Perugia is still a city of weathered stone buildings and dark medieval streets that curve and tilt downhill with sudden precipitous drops; of narrow archways and climbing staircases that open unexpectedly onto a view of the gentle landscape below. Here and there Renaissance and baroque palazzi lighten the medieval fabric of the city, but a single tower is all that remains of the original seventy that thrust upward "like the fingers of a man's hand," according to Alberti. The city's main piazza and the Corso Vannucci beyond are always full of students lounging against the steps of the Cathedral and of crowds strolling the elegant central street. Light washes across the shop windows full of stylish clothing, fine leathers, and pastries, while nearby are such dark narrow arteries as the Via dell Gabbia, where criminals once hung in cages from the Palazzo dei

Priori, and the Via delle Volte, which is roofed over by the blackened arches of stone vaults. *Case pensili,* hanging houses that bridge the space between those on either side, create dramatic patterns of light and shade on the cobbled paths below.

From below the town, the steep arc of the Via Appia with its long, lyric flow of stairs leads into the central piazza, Quattro Novembre, which in turn opens into the Corso Vannucci, the meeting place of Perugia.

In the violet haze of evening, the *passeggiata,* the promenade, finds hundreds of Perugians strolling its undulating plane, from the unadorned Cathedral at one end to the ramparts overlooking the entire Tiber Valley at the other. The street's profile is bold and romantic, with overlapping roofs silhouetted against the sensuous curves of the buildings. Clearly intended for the pleasures of walking, the Corso Vannucci is now closed to automobile traffic. Friends meet, women shop, and businessmen gather over coffee, free from the intrusion of the car.

At the center of the square is an elaborately designed fountain with sculptures in relief by Nicola and Giovanni Pisano. The exuberant bas-reliefs of the lower basin celebrate the rhythms of the medieval year—in the sowing and tilling of crops, the harvesting of grapes, and the hunting of game—while the more restrained sculptures of the upper depict the life and society of the time with historical and biblical figures. At the top of this marble mountain, sculpted to celebrate the triumphant arrival of water such a great distance from the sea, rise three bronze nymphs, consummate examples of the Gothic sculptor's art. The red and white stone of the Palazzo Comunale, or Palazzo dei Priori, the massive Town Hall, defines one edge of the asymmetrical square with rhythmic semicircular stairs leading to a great portal. It is an unmistakable expression of civic power and strength, built long before the Perugians—who were supposed to be the Popes' major Umbrian allies—even constructed the Cathedral, which remains unfinished to this day. Pink and white marble covers only the lower part; the weathered raw bricks above now create perfect perching space for the hundreds of pigeons that circle overhead and alight in the piazza. The much larger Palazzo Comunale holds not only the municipal offices but also the public library, the National Gallery of Umbria, and the Audience Hall of the Mercantile College. The

building itself curves and undulates down the Corso Vannucci with swellings that suggest the churches, towers, and houses it absorbed in its own expansion. Immediately adjacent is the Collegio del Cambio, the seat of the town's money changers, decorated with frescoes by Perugino.

For all its medieval character, Perugia is rooted in a far earlier time, as its Etruscan walls and arched gateways bear witness. Dating from the classical period is the tomb known as the Ipogeo dei Volumni, dug deep into the soft tufa at the southeastern edge of the city. Inside is an almost precise replica of an Etruscan-Roman house with burial urns of an aristocratic family. In the most elaborately decorated chamber, the patriarch of the illustrious family lies on a couch, supported by two winged Furies whose stern faces bear an extraordinary resemblance to sculptures by Michelangelo, thus serving as powerful reminders of the classical roots of the Renaissance.

On a grassy hillside edged with slender cypresses near the crenellated medieval gate of Sant' Angelo, at the farthest northern reach of the city, is the early Christian Church of San Michele Arcangelo, one of the few that survived the barbarian assaults. Built in the fifth century with material salvaged from pagan buildings, it has a circular plan like that of the Pantheon in Rome, although its roof rests on a ring of Corinthian columns that encircle the ancient altar.

Standing on a hilltop to the south is the church of San Pietro, built in the tenth century on the site of an early cathedral, its antique pillars rising chastely in a dark interior weighted with the sumptuous gilding of later eras. It was twice converted to use as a fortress, once in the fourteenth century and once when Benedictine monks joined the resistance to an assault by papal troops sent to crush a popular rebellion.

From the days of the Etruscans, the relationship of Perugia to Rome alternated between sympathy and rebellion. Octavian treated the inhabitants with ferocity when they sided with Mark Antony against him in the civil war after the assassination of Julius Caesar, and they responded by destroying half the town rather than give in. Octavian retaliated with a winter siege that starved the populace into submission, and then executed three hundred of the town's leading citizens. After he became the emperor Augustus, Octavian rebuilt the city and carved the inscription *Augusta Perusia* that can still be seen on the Etruscan arch that overlooks the Piazza Fortebraccio; but Perugia has no sign of a Roman temple, amphitheater, forum, or baths.

Perugia appeared above us, crowning a mighty hill, the most picturesque of cities; and the higher we ascended, the more the view opened before us, as we looked back on the course we had traversed, and saw the wide valley, sweeping down and spreading out, bounded afar by mountains and sleeping in sun and shadow. No language nor any art of the pencil can give an idea of the scene. When God expressed himself in the landscape to mankind, He did not intend that it should be translated into any tongue save his own immediate one.

NATHANIEL HAWTHORNE
French and Italian Notebooks

Fruit picker

The ground in this valley is very fertile and further on the hillsides things are highly cultivated, and inhabited; they are so covered with olive trees that you could not see anything more beautiful, seeing that among these small hills there are sometimes very high mountains, which you see to be cultivated to the very summit, and very fertile with all kinds of fruit.

MICHEL MONTAIGNE
Diary of a Journey to Italy

Like every other town in Umbria, Perugia suffered under the barbarian invasions. It took Totila seven years to subdue the city; at the end, when there was mass starvation behind the walls, the bishop Herculanus urged resistance, and at his suggestion the last sheep was fattened, slaughtered, and thrown over the walls, in the hope of suggesting such reserves of food that a single sheep meant nothing. The ruse failed, and Totila devastated Perugia, ordering a particularly horrible execution for the valiant bishop. The siege is depicted in a lively fresco by Benedetto Bonfigli that hangs in the National Gallery of Umbria, where the medieval look of the town is preserved in minutely observed architectural detail.

By 1321 Perugia had outgrown its Etruscan walls, and the building of a second circuit of ramparts, between four and five miles in circumference, began. Despite efforts to establish a papal state in central Italy, the Perugians' independent spirit repeatedly asserted itself. Five popes were elected in conclaves at Perugia; but of several who came there to escape turmoil in Rome, two died of poisoning; another, Martin IV, who had earlier excommunicated the city for the destruction of nearby Foligno, met his end from eating too many eels, presumably taken from Lake Trasimeno. During the Middle Ages the city was the most powerful in Umbria and made war against Assisi, Spoleto, Gubbio,

Siena, and Città di Castello. Its walls with their square crenellations indicate allegiance to the Guelph cause, while all over the surrounding countryside the swallow-tail shapes at the tops of buildings showed adherence to the Ghibellines and suggest constant conflict with the Perugians.

But Perugia was also riven with internal struggles. The *condottiere* Braccio Fortebraccio, who controlled the city for eight years, revived the old game of *la battaglia dei sassi* (the battle of stones) as the way of deflecting the city's aggressive energies. In it rival teams divided between the heavily armed, padded, and helmeted *armati* and the lightly protected *lanciatori* fought for control of a piazza. The *armati* massed in the center of the square while their opponents showered them with rocks and stones and tried to drive them back. The game began at dawn, and by sunset, after as many as two thousand men had taken part, there were often twenty or more who had been maimed, wounded, or left for dead on the field. Fortebraccio began his career by defeating the forces of the Pope in a conflict immortalized by Paolo Uccello's famous picture *The Battle of San Romano,* and when he died in southeastern Umbria, the Popes once again took charge in Perugia. All that remains of the palace he built for himself is the elegant loggia next to the façade of the Duomo, but in dying he left the city an unforgettable memorial, for it was his successor, Pope Martin V, whose favoritism set the Baglioni family in power.

John Addington Symonds wrote in *Sketches and Studies in Italy and Greece* of how "in Perugia both the martial violence and the religious sentiment of medievalism were raised for a minute to the elevation of high art." Savagery reached a peak under the rule of the despotic Baglioni, when churches were used as fortresses and brothers massacred one another. In their conspiracy of the summer of 1500, these Baglioni—with dramatic names like Atalanta, Grifone, Zenobia, and Astorre—turned upon one another and allowed their darkest instincts full range. The city witnessed a vendetta so terrible that the Cathedral had to be washed with wine to rid it of the blood that had profaned its stones. Soon afterward, Pope Paul III sent his army to destroy the family and tear down its strongholds, on whose ruins he commissioned the architect Antonio da Sangallo to build a new fortress, the Rocca Paolina; the inscription above one of its gateways reads *Ad coercendam Peru-sinorum audaciam* (for the repression of Perugian audacity). The great arch and crown of the Etruscan Porta Marzia, from the second or third century B.C.,

were incorporated into the brickwork of the Rocca and today look down over the frantic rush of modern traffic. Although the Perugians hated the fortress and managed to destroy most of it in 1860, when the town was at last freed from papal rule, what still remains forms a sub-structure of the Piazza Italia. Below it runs the Via Baglioni, an Umbrian Pompeii where the houses of the family are now vacant, cold, and silent, with bricked-up windows and ghostly arcades leading nowhere.

This city of violence was also the home of Pietro Vannucci, who took the name Perugino (the Perugian) and set his devotional paintings in the soft Umbrian countryside. His compositions express the lyrical side of Perugia and invite the eye to wander through a land-scape filled with low hills, feathery trees, and sunlight warming the cool, silvery air. Raphael came to study with him at the impressionable age of sixteen. Although little remains of Raphael's own work in Perugia, the influence of his teacher on his paintings is unmistakable.

The religious impulse of the Perugians expressed itself, not in the gentle humanism of St. Francis, but rather in the *battuti,* the flagellants who whipped them-selves until the blood flowed as an act of penance. When the Franciscan St. Bernardino of Siena preached from the doorway of the Duomo, calling on the Perugians to burn all their books and luxurious posses-sions, he moved them with his denunciations of vio-lence, although they often left him to return to their harrowing battles. To him they dedicated the elegant Oratory of San Bernardino with its intricately carved façade by Agostino di Duccio. The oratory stands in a field where the Franciscans used to preach, next to the tall church of San Francesco, whose outer wall is a Byzantine profusion of geometric designs in pink and white marble. Today, because of shifts in the unstable earth, it stands without a roof, a mere shell of the original structure, which was modeled on the upper church of the basilica in Assisi. Set peacefully on its grassy lawn edged with a row of pines, the Franciscan church belies the extreme rivalry between Perugia and Assisi, the city of St. Francis. After he died, the Perugians in fact tried to snatch the saint's body during the funeral procession, and his followers had to hide it deep in the foundations of the great basilica at Assisi, where it lay undisturbed, and indeed undiscovered, until the nineteenth century.

Perugia remains the most intensely urban of all Umbrian hill towns. Its famous university, which was founded in 1200 and granted university status in 1308, continues to attract an enormous number of students,

Via Mazzini, Perugia

while thousands of foreigners enroll at the Università Italiana per Stranieri (the University for Foreigners) to learn Italian and study the culture. The student population is so sizable that at almost any hour of day or night students can be found in the Piazza Quattro Novembre lounging against the cathedral steps, tossing Frisbees, playing guitars, or strolling. The entire development of Italian art can be traced at Perugia, from its prehistoric and Etruscan beginnings in the Museo Archeologico Nazionale through the paintings in the Byzantine and Sienese-Umbrian style, the work of the great Tuscans—Fra Angelico, Piero della Francesca, Benozzo Gozzoli—and that of the Umbrians Perugino and Pinturicchio. Within these city walls past and present play off against each other as Vespas and Fiats whiz through the narrow medieval streets, past towering Etruscan gates, and through piazze that pulsate with the energy of the present.

During the heyday of the Grand Tour, few travelers ventured up the forbiddingly steep road to Perugia.

One who did was Tobias Smollett—and though he tended toward dyspeptic grumbling, he pronounced himself well pleased with the place. Henry James was entranced with Perugia's traditions but disdainful of the contemporary refurbishing. He wrote in *Italian Hours*, "The castle is being completely *remis à neuf* . . . a Massachusetts schoolhouse couldn't suggest a briefer yesterday." During a trip to Italy in 1921 Theodore Dreiser, in *A Traveler at Forty,* described Perugia as "the most remarkable, the most sparkling, the most forward in all things commercial." Aldous Huxley's evocative description of the city in his novel *Those Barren Leaves,* after a trip through the hill towns in 1923, reflects his obvious pleasure in the city. Although to some Perugia was chiefly notable because it was the home of the teacher of Raphael, Huxley's own response echoed that of Henry James, who observed after a week there, "I had had enough of Perugia, but had not had enough of the view."

From the gentle Umbrian plain, Assisi appears as a splash of white spilling lightly down the hillside. No dark medieval presence with towers piercing the sky, it is all soft pinks and grays, its buildings formed of the rosy limestone of Monte Subasio, whose slopes rise starkly behind it. The city is anchored to its hillside by the massive two-tiered Basilica of St. Francis, marching upward on enormous double arches— a religious fortress grander even than the citadel rising above the town. Yet neither monumental church nor massive Rocca at the top of the hill can detract from Assisi's dreamy, welcoming character. Today the crumbling castle is a reminder of the times when it was the stronghold of whichever despot ruled the city. Assisi had been overrun by Totila the Goth and had later been subject to the Dukes of Spoleto, but in 1198 the people tore down the castle these overlords had built and used its stone for ramparts of their own. It was not quite two centuries later that the Cardinal Albornoz constructed the building to which Pope Paul III eventually added the huge cylindrical tower that looks directly over the town.

On the summit, the upper church shoots up as brilliant, as aerial, as triumphantly, as this is low and grave. Really, if one were to give way to conjecture, he might suppose that in these three sanctuaries the architect meant to represent the three worlds; below, the gloom of death and the horrors of the infernal tomb; in the middle, the impassioned anxiety of the beseeching Christian who strives and hopes in this world of trial; aloft, the bliss and dazzling glory of paradise.

HIPPOLYTE TAINE
Italy

In the valley below, the great dome of Santa Maria degli Angeli dominates the landscape and enfolds the Porziuncola, the little chapel where St. Francis died. Every year, buses full of tourists and pilgrims pause here and then rumble on up and through the Porta San Pietro to pay homage to St. Francis. As many as two million of them come annually, but the city remains essentially as it was in medieval times and its soft colors and luminous setting still preserve some reminder of his gentle spirit. Even the narrow stone alleys that climb up and down from the piazza are consistently brightened by splashes of geraniums and carnations in window boxes and on wrought-iron balconies. The steep winding rhythms of these narrow passageways are a counterpoint to the wider streets that stretch in parallel lines across the contour of the hill. The main street sweeps in a diagonal arc to the golden Basilica with its grassy lawn and curves past medieval houses with stone balconies and coats of arms, past the town library with its Gregorian chants and papal bulls, and past postcard and souvenir vendors who are even more numerous than the fountains at almost every corner.

St. Francis was born Giovanni, son of Bernardone, a rich textile merchant, and his youth was full of high-spirited entertainments. He went off to fight in one of

Assisi's perennial battles against the Perugians, but he was captured and imprisoned for a year in a Perugian jail. He seemed untouched by the experience, but it was after an illness brought him near death that he transformed himself into Signor Poverello, who, as he put it, fell in love with Lady Poverty. In a time of intense personal confusion, he prayed for guidance at the crumbling sanctuary of San Damiano, outside the town, and heard the crucifix above the altar tell him to rebuild the church. Francis sold cloth from his father's warehouse to finance repairs, and for this act of filial disobedience he was permanently estranged from his family. Choosing to live by the precepts of the Gospel, he dressed in a rough gray habit tied by a rope around the waist and began walking barefoot through the countryside, where his words touched the hearts of his listeners.

As his following grew and when Pope Innocent III sanctioned his order, the Benedictines gave him the Porziuncola, or "Little Portion," a tiny chapel on the plain originally preserved by St. Benedict in the sixth century. He built simple huts for his first followers and from this spot, with its little chapel open to the sky, Francis walked and preached all over Umbria. In a time of superstition, violence, and corruption within the Church, the people of Umbria responded to the naturalness and simplicity of Francis himself, and to the mercy and humanity of his vision. He died in 1226 and was canonized just two years later. On the day after the canonization, Pope Gregory IX laid the foundation stone for the Basilica at Assisi. It is ironic that a saint who had dedicated his life to the austere ideals of early Christianity should be memorialized by so imposing and materialistic a monument; but such an outpouring of donations arrived to finance it that the lower church was completed in twenty-two months, and the upper church received its roof six years later.

The lower church is low-roofed, cavernous, and dark, its dense vaults and forest of arches ornamented with frescoes and geometrical designs. They cover every visible surface and play off against the patterned floor, chapels, and clusters of columns. The walls are like a richly illustrated storybook, a missal for the senses, where the biblical narrative and lives of the saints are portrayed by Cimabue, Simone Martini, Giotto, and

We are in the lower church of S. Francesco. High mass is being sung, with orchestra and organ and a choir of many voices. Candles are lighted on the altar, over-canopied with Giotto's allegories. From the low southern windows slants the sun, in narrow bands, upon the many-coloured gloom and embrowned glory of these painted aisles. . . . The whole low-vaulted building glows duskily; the frescoed roof, the stained windows, the figure-crowded pavements blending their rich but subdued colours, like hues upon some marvelous moth's wings, or like a deep-toned rainbow mist discerned in twilight dreams, or like such tapestry as Eastern queens, in ancient days, wrought for the pavilion of an empress. . . . Each face is a poem; the counterpart in painting to a chapter from the Fioretti di San Francesco.

JOHN ADDINGTON SYMONDS
Sketches and Studies in Italy and Greece

Pietro Lorenzetti. The French philosopher Hippolyte Taine considered it "the masterpiece of mystic Christianity" and wrote of the lower church that he would not change "this cavern for all the churches of Rome." Buried still deeper in the crypt, beneath the lower church, lies the body of the saint.

To move from the darkness of the lower church to the vast, light-filled upper level is to be dazzled by a single lofty space, where the radiance of golden light pours in to illumine the drama of its frescoes. Here, too, every inch of the walls has been painted, including all five vaults of the ceiling and the apse behind the altar. In the transept the frescoes of Cimabue, many of them now faded to an outline, show the beginning of a departure from the Byzantine tradition toward a more natural human feeling; the monk bowed with grief at the foot of Cimabue's scene of the Crucifixion is St. Francis himself. And in telling the story of the actual St. Francis, a man who had lived and died in Assisi not many years before, the frescoes of Giotto were truly revolutionary. In painting him in the Umbrian countryside with the animals and the birds of the field and the little walled towns on the hills, Giotto (or his students and assistants, or himself with their help, for controversy surrounds the authorship of the works) showed himself profoundly sympathetic to the spirit of the saint. Just as Dante wrote in the vernacular of his time, Giotto painted the world as he saw it, not according to formal convention. After Francis, religion became more personal, centering on the humanity of Jesus, Mary, and the saints. As Paul Sabatier observes in his biography of St. Francis, "The thirteenth century was ready to understand the voice of the poet of Umbria; the sermon to the birds signalled the end of the reign of Byzantine art and the ideas it symbolized. It signalled the end of dogmatism and authority; the arrival of individualism and inspiration."

Even more than in the art that commemorated it, the real spirit of St. Francis is to be found outside the walls of the Basilica. Sheltered in a grove of olive trees near the edge of Assisi stands San Damiano, the chapel that St. Francis first repaired, stone by stone, and later made into the convent of the Poor Clares, the female counterpart of his own religious order. It was here that he came, near the end of his life, blind and ill, to be cared for by the nuns, and here, it is said, that he wrote his "Canticle to the Sun." In this intimate sanctuary, with its tiny rough-hewn chapel and tiny plot of garden, much more than at the grander moments, St. Francis's warmth and gentleness can still be felt.

Lower Basilica of St. Francis, Assisi

Detail, Duomo, San Rufino, Assisi

Sunrise, Upper Basilica of St. Francis, Assisi

The spirit of the saint is more profoundly present in the hermitage of the Carceri, hidden among the oak forests higher on the slope of Monte Subasio. Here St. Francis often went in search of solitude, when the hermitage was merely a series of caves. A convent was built here by St. Bernardino in the fifteenth century, and despite many new additions, the spare simplicity and peacefulness remain.

St. Francis's presence is everywhere. It has eclipsed that of the Roman poet Propertius, who was also a native of Assisi, but when Goethe traveled to the city in 1786 St. Francis was decidedly not the attraction. The poet turned away from the great Basilica, which he described as "forbidding" and like a "Babylonian tower," and made straight for the classical Temple of Minerva. This graceful shrine, with its six slender Corinthian columns, has stood in the main piazza since the time of

Augustus and is the city's most famous Roman relic. It is now a Christian church that dominates the square, while a fountain bubbles nearby and a thirteenth-century town hall across from it shelters a café with umbrella-shaded tables before it. The Romans, who named the city Asisium, built their forum here. In the northernmost part of town, where the amphitheater now stands, there was once a citadel, and beyond the oak-shaded public gardens are the remnants of arches and baths dating to Roman times.

The handsome Romanesque Duomo of San Rufino is named for the first bishop of Assisi, who was martyred here in the third century, and it may first have been a Roman temple. Enlarged in the eleventh century, it plays a relatively minor role in the ceremony of this Franciscan town. Its façade is richly carved with animals whose tawny shapes are thrown into high relief

Column and staircase detail, Upper Basilica of St. Francis, Assisi

There is a world here as in an animated forest, and each object is complex, complete like a living thing; on one hand is the choir-stalls, surcharged and sown with sculptures; yonder a rich winding staircase, elaborate railings, a light marble pulpit and funeral monuments, the marble which fretted and chased, seems the most elegant jewel-casket: all this vaguely discernible in a dim purple light, amidst dark reflections from the wainscottings, whilst, at the entrance, the setting sun radiates myriads of golden darts like the peacock displaying its splendor.

HIPPOLYTE TAINE
Italy

Intarsia, Upper Basilica of St. Francis, Assisi

If, with Goethe I were to balance anything against the attractions of the double church I should choose the ruined castle on the hill above the town. . . . The castle is a splendid piece of ruin, perched on the summit of the mountain to whose slope Assisi clings and dropping a pair of stony arms to enclose the little town in its embrace. The city wall, in other words, straggles up the steep green hill and meets the crumbling skeleton of the fortress.

HENRY JAMES
A Chain of Cities

by the rays of the late afternoon sun as they surround the rose window and support a fine gallery of arches. The red marble lions at the door with their tightly curled manes sit as impassively as they did for the baptisms of St. Francis, St. Clare, and even Frederick II, whose plans for imperial conquest were thwarted by the monk who treated birds of the air with the same dignity that he accorded monarchs and popes.

Because of such associations, Assisi is the scene of many festivals and religious ceremonies. Pilgrims are drawn, often from great distances, for Holy Week, which begins in the Cathedral with a reenactment of the Deposition, moves to the Basilica in a dramatic torch-lit procession through the streets, then returns to the Cathedral. At the festival of Calendimaggio on April 30 and May 1, singers and other musicians in medieval dress wind through the town, singing ancient chivalric songs, just as St. Francis did in his youth. The festival is as much a celebration of the rites of spring as it is an evocation of religion, with girls carrying cascades of flowers, boys dressed in bright medieval costumes, and banners ruffled by breezes and flapping against the stone buildings. At the Pardon of Assisi, from July 31 through August 2, pilgrims in traditional costume, some of whom have walked many miles barefoot, make their way from the heights of the Carceri past all the Franciscan monuments, on their way to the Porziuncola inside the great church of Santa Maria degli Angeli on the plain. Another local holiday is the Festa del Voto, celebrating the miracle of St. Clare, when—as legend has it— she went boldly forth to meet the armed hordes of Saracens sent by Frederick to destroy the city. They are said to have been so unnerved by the sight of the young woman that they fled, and Assisi was spared. On the night of June 21 the entire town is lit by thousands of torches; at dawn the next morning the bells ring to commemorate the hour of the event and a procession of Franciscans and townspeople in medieval dress makes its way to San Damiano, while trumpeters play the ancient city hymn on long silver horns. The greatest throngs of all come on October 3 and 4, for the Transito di San Francesco. To commemorate the death and apotheosis of the saint, there is a simple service at dusk before the saint's tomb in the crypt, while outside the city glows with the hundreds of candles whose flickering light gives it a look of timeless antiquity.

When Theodore Dreiser reached Assisi and read St. Francis's vow of poverty, he was electrified. It "made my hair tingle to the roots," he wrote. Gabriele D'Annunzio, the flamboyant poet, cult figure, and Fascist ideologue, wrote a series of lyric poems during his long involvement with the actress Eleonora Duse, of which the *Elettra* group dealt with a number of Tuscan and Umbrian hill towns. He called them "Cities of Silence," and the lines on Assisi contain vigorous images that convey a bold sense of the place. D. H. Lawrence is one of the few travelers to dislike Assisi. "I can't stand Saint Francis," he wrote to Dorothy Brett in 1926, "—nor St. Clare—nor St. Catherine. I don't even like Assisi. They've killed so much of the precious interchange of life; most folks are half dead, maimed, because of those blighters. The indecency of sprinkling good food with ashes and dirtying sensitive mouths."

Gertrude Stein, on the other hand, liked Assisi very much; she insisted on arriving there on foot from Perugia, traveling as St. Francis had once, and whimsically pictured herself in old age as one of the women of Assisi who led beribboned black pigs up and down the hills. Mark Schorer, in "The Unwritten Story," evoked the Umbrian sunshine as it poured over the entire Spoletan valley, where the silvery river Chiascio winding to meet the Tiber glistens in a landscape that St. Francis saw as a kind of paradise. As seen from the great Basilica, or from the stone balustrades of the neighboring Hotel Subasio with their pots of geraniums, it still looks like a garden whose poplars make pointillist patterns against the green and golden squares of the countryside.

Gertrude Stein was very fond of Assisi for two reasons, because of Saint Francis and the beauty of his city and because the old women used to lead instead of a goat a little pig up and down the hills of Assisi. The little black pig was always decorated with a red ribbon. Gertrude Stein had always liked little pigs and she always said that in her old age she expected to wander up and down the hills of Assisi with a little black pig.

GERTRUDE STEIN
The Autobiography of Alice B. Toklas

Rocca Maggiore, Assisi

Orvieto

Suspended on its pedestal of honey-colored stone nine hundred feet above the countryside, Orvieto looks almost illusory, a towered and pinnacled Magritte-like city on a flat slab of rock rising above the valley mists. The platform of rock on which it rests is volcanic stone, once covered with lava and ash, a remnant of the earthquakes and volcanic convulsions that lifted it out of the water that flooded the surrounding plain. The original Etruscan settlers saw those steep-sided cliffs as a natural fortress, and none of its later conquerors—Roman, Goth, or Lombard—ever felt the need to encircle the isolated site with defensive walls.

Orvieto, which is only seventy-five miles from Rome, beckons the traveler up a road that loops past medieval buildings of the same tawny color, past shops where the pale straw-colored wines of Orvieto are sold, into a narrow piazza where the somber horizontal stripes of black basalt and white travertine along the sides of the Duomo give no hint of the exuberance of its famous façade.

That façade is a blazing explosion of marble and mosaic, of rosy pinks and dazzling golds, a profusion of sculptured carvings and bas-reliefs, of niches and galleries enclosed in a riot of twisting spiral columns. Charles Eliot Norton described it as "the illuminated page of a marble missal." Its giant triptych form frames three hundred years of art that includes intricate tracery and delicately carved sculpture as well as the sculpted stories of the Old and New Testament on the pilasters between the doors that begin with lyrical dreamlike figures from the Creation and end in brutal scenes of violence at an awesome Last Judgment. After the brilliant color and lavish ornament of the exterior, the interior is a shock, a cool plunge into the world of the spirit. Light passes through stained-glass windows and panels of alabaster and illuminates a seemingly immense space where pillars banded with black and white stand as tall as enormous trees rooted in a silent kingdom.

Begun in the Romanesque style when Orvieto was one of the most prosperous cities in central Italy, and given its Gothic form by Lorenzo Maitani one

Duomo, Orvieto

Detail, wall, Via Maitani, Orvieto

hundred years later, the Duomo dominates the city. It stands at the highest point of Orvieto, where an Etruscan temple is said to have been centuries before, and was built to celebrate the Miracle of Bolsena. According to reports, a young Bohemian priest was traveling to Rome beset with doubts about whether the body of Christ was really present in the holy wafer. Along the way he celebrated Mass in a church on the shores of Lake Bolsena, and as he broke the Host, he saw it exude drops of blood, which fell and stained the altar cloth. News of the miracle quickly reached Pope Urban IV, who was in nearby Orvieto at the time—having come, as many popes would continue to do, to escape the political intrigues and summer heat of Rome—and who seized the opportunity to reestablish one of the most profound tenets of Roman Catholic belief. He commemorated the miracle by establishing the feast of Corpus Christi, which celebrates the vindication of the dogma of transubstantiation, and called on Thomas Aquinas to compose the sacred office of the day.

Since 1264 it has been celebrated every year on August 15 with a festival and procession through the city. Banners drape all the major buildings and a colorful parade of costumed trumpeters, knights, squires, and pages walks before the sacred chalice cloth, carried inside an elaborate gold and enamel reliquary whose shape is a miniature replica of the façade of Duomo. At all other times the reliquary remains within the Cathedral, where two chapels offer emblematic views of the changing world of the early Renaissance. In one hangs Lippo Memmi's delicate Sienese *Madonna* along with the reliquary, which is a symbol of medieval faith. Directly opposite stands the chapel begun with frescoes by Fra Angelico and Benozzo Gozzoli and completed thirty years later by Luca Signorelli with the force of a Dantesque vision of the end of the world and its attendant horrors. In one scene of the damned in a dense, airless hell, naked figures are bound, strangled, and tortured by ghastly colored demons whose great wings and twisted horns do not conceal their basic human form. They set upon their victims, garroting them and tearing at their flesh before hurling them to the crowded ground below. Damnation and pain are set against joy in a scene of the resurrection of the flesh in which exhausted and bewildered people return to life, emerging from the gray ground of death, littered with remnants of bony skeletons. Signorelli investigated the human form with an unsparing eye, and within this single chapel indicated the beginnings of our sense of

our earthly powers and potentialities. He took such a leap of daring that, according to Vasari, Michelangelo came here to study his portrayal of the human body, and drew on what he had learned from it for his own frescoes for the Sistine Chapel in the Vatican.

From the laying of the first stone of the cathedral in 1290, appalling amounts of human blood were shed in realizing the dream of civic grandeur and religious devotion. When Orvieto was not at war with Todi, Perugia, Viterbo, or Siena, there were feuds and conspiracies of the Monaldeschi and Filippeschi families, the leading Guelphs and Ghibellines whose vendettas were so virulent that Dante compared them to the Montagues and Capulets. After the Monaldeschi family had finally won out, its members promptly turned against one another, splitting into four factions known as the Deer, Dog, Eagle, and Viper, of which, appropriately, the Viper was both the most treacherous and most successful. The brief triumph of its faction was cut short by the Plague of 1348, which left Orvieto a collection of ruins dominated by its Cathedral.

The city was so weakened that it became prey to mercenary armies, expansionist nobles, and finally to the Church itself. At the end of the thirteenth century Pope Martin IV had settled there with numbers of Franciscans; and in 1528, a year after the sack of Rome by the emperor Charles V, Clement VII fled to Orvieto. Realizing that in the event of a protracted siege the city would need water, he commissioned Antonio da Sangallo to design what came to be known as the Well of San Patrizio (St. Patrick). To bring up water from springs a hundred feet below the surface, two separate spiral staircases, each forty feet wide, were cut into the rock, forming a double corridor wide enough to allow the passage of donkeys and mules. The entrance and exit are still to be seen near the public gardens, beside the crumbling battlements of the Rocca. The building of this fortress was begun in 1364, on the orders of Cardinal Albornoz, the ubiquitous papal legate, as an addition to the string of military defenses he had already set in place across the Umbrian landscape.

Across the square from the Duomo, in the Palazzo Faina, Greek and Etruscan objects give evidence of the city's ancient beginnings. One of the last Etruscan cities to be conquered by the Romans, Orvieto may have been given its name as citizens fled to another site, atop a nearby hill, leaving behind the *urbs vetus,* or old city—whence Orvieto—to keep a silent watch. Almost no relic remains from Roman times. During the eleventh and twelfth centuries, after being successively plundered by Goths, Byzantines, and Lombards, Orvieto began the rebuilding of the city we see today.

Narrow streets leave the Piazza del Duomo, with its shops selling bright ceramics and wines of the region, and wind circuitously to the Palazzo del Popolo. An ecclesiastical palace before it became the seat of the Captain of the People, the palazzo is a monument of civic consciousness whose powerful form is softened by elegant triple-pierced windows, by curves rippling above the open arches at its base, and by the sinuous turn of its merlons. From its balcony the piazza below looks like a sea of bright colors as canvas umbrellas shade the town market with its stands thick with fruits, vegetables, and flowers.

The Piazza della Repubblica, which was probably the Etruscan and Roman forum, is still the center of Orvieto. On one side of this mammoth square stands the Palazzo Comunale, with fine Renaissance windows above a base that remains unfinished to this day, with a single fragment of uncompleted arch arrested in midair. Traffic passes under one of its deep arches to join a network of tiny, twisting streets. The shadow of the adjacent twelve-sided Campanile falls over the Church of Sant' Andrea, first built in the sixth century over subterranean traces of an Etruscan structure and rebuilt in Romanesque times. It has a long connection with the papacy and with medieval history. Here Innocent III announced the formation of the Fourth Crusade, Martin IV was crowned Pope in 1281, and Pope Nicholas IV and Boniface VIII were both made cardinals.

The piazza stands at the edge of the medieval quarter, a maze of quiet streets curving around a handful of churches and low-roofed houses. Arches connect palazzi on either side of the street, and plants in pots are everywhere—balanced on terrace railings, leaning against the bases of Romanesque and Renaissance columns, and even wired to building fronts, lyric spots of color against the monochromatic stone. Streets winding their way to the edge of the rock pass ancient buildings transformed to modern uses, including churches that have been turned into garages or restaurants with dramatic settings and spectacular views. One church that has not been altered is San Giovenale, whose dark tufa façade and stumpy tower give little hint of its glowing interior, with frescoed walls and columns, and its altar carved with symbols of the four Evangelists—angel (Matthew), lion (Mark), bull (Luke), and eagle (John). Outside it stand the city walls, where the ancient gateway of the Porta Maggiore marks a natural cleft in

the rock that the Etruscans first used as a point of access.

Monumental Etruscan tombs have been discovered directly below the town, along with the wine cellars used by the Etruscans. They carried out the entire wine-making process here, crushing and fermenting the grapes at an upper level and aging the wine in cool, deep tunnels that pierce the rock below. Orvieto's crisp, dry, or slightly sweet white wines, very different from the sweet wines famous in Renaissance times, still come from grapes cultivated in the fertile valley below the town.

Over thousands of years the action of water carved the porous tufa of the cliff with chasms and fissures, and the Etruscans further undermined it with their tunnels and drainage channels. Later medieval sewers and tunnels have now dangerously eroded the foundation of the rock, and the precipice is crumbling. Vegetation grows in large vertical cracks, and landslides have removed chunks of garden and walls. The vibration of traffic continues to undermine the tufa, but major reconstruction has now consolidated the rock.

The countryside that stretches at the foot of Orvieto is cut through by the Paglia River and includes untamed woods that shelter boar and wildcats as well as the elegantly restored Romanesque Abbey of Sts. Martin and Stephen, which has been transformed into a hotel, La Badia, for travelers to Orvieto.

Before the mid-nineteenth century, however, it was a rare traveler who braved the ascent of the town's precipitous cliffs. John Addington Symonds wrote in *Sketches and Studies in Italy and Greece* that Orvieto appeared "forbidding and terrible" with its menacing castle and desolate, thinly populated streets. "You might think Orvieto had been stricken for its sins by Heaven. Your mind would dwell mechanically on all that you have read of Papal crimes, of fratricidal war, of Pagan abominations in the high places of the Church, of tempestuous passions and refined iniquity—of everything, in fact, which rendered Italy of the Middle Ages and the Renaissance dark and ominous amid the splendors of her art and civilization."

In 1828 the painter J. M. W. Turner, who was to spend two years in Italy, produced a painting of Orvieto which, according to one of his biographers, "challenged the very sun in its splendor." Charles Eliot Norton, who decided to devote his life to art and literature after reading Ruskin's *Modern Painters,* responded to the art of the Middle Ages and rejected that of the Renaissance as being a time of "degraded taste and debasing principles." When he got to Orvieto, he observed the dark

Chapel, La Badia

Interior, Duomo, Orvieto

and dirty streets, whose shrunken and deserted aspect, he thought, made the Cathedral even more brilliant by contrast. He spent weeks chronicling the construction of the Cathedral, and although he hated the pagan past, he noted with enthusiasm that the richest of its marbles came from pagan Rome, whence they were distributed for use in the building of Christian churches. He wrote of how bands of citizens harnessed themselves to wagons filled with these materials and dragged them up the steep cliff, after first confessing their sins and, presumably, leaving all their angry and hateful feelings behind.

The painter Augustus John went to Orvieto to pay "homage to Mantegna and Signorelli and did not fail to sample the wine for which this town is also celebrated." Though the Signorelli and the wine are still in evidence, no record of the Mantegna is to be found.

Roger Fry, who would become the most influential art critic in England after Ruskin, left home as a young man of twenty-five after breaking with his family over his decision to become an artist. He wrote of Orvieto that he saw it "under rather unfavorable circumstances. But it is a grand place. I have been retracting all the evil things I have ever said about Gothic, and this is just after seeing Paestum, where Doric architecture is at its best, so that my standard should be high."

Twenty thousand people lived in Orvieto at the end of the thirteenth century, when the building of its Cathedral began. Today about the same number of inhabitants walk these narrow streets, over stones worn smooth by the centuries, and join the *passeggiata* at the end of the day beneath the golden mosaics of Duomo, maintaining the continuity of a city whose roots are sunk deep in the time of the Etruscans.

Orvieto

Imagine a rock in the midst of a melan-
choly valley, and on the top of the rock a
city so deathly silent as to give the impres-
sion of being uninhabited—every window
closed, grass growing in the dusty grey
streets. A Capuchin friar crosses the
Piazza, a priest descends from a closed
carriage in front of a hospital, all in black,
with a decrepit old servant to open the
door; here a tower against the white, rain-
sodden clouds, there a clock slowly striking
the hour, and suddenly, at the end of the
street, a miracle—the Duomo.

GABRIELE D'ANNUNZIO

Legend has it that Todi was originally laid out not at
the peak of its steep hill but on the plain below, until an
eagle swooped down, seized the plan in its talons,
and dropped it along the crown of the hill. Taking this
as an omen from the gods, the first Umbrian settlers
proceeded to build on the spot where the ruined
medieval fortress stands today, overlooking the river and
the gently rolling Tiber Valley. The eagle has remained
the emblem of Todi. A great bronze bird spreads its
wings across the front of the Palazzo dei Priori, and
smaller versions appear on walls, gates, and doors
throughout the city. The spearheads, daggers, and
hatchets of polished stone found in nearby tombs cross
the frontier of myth as tangible evidence of the
settlement's antiquity.

Today Todi is ringed by three sets of walls and
gates, showing how the city grew from one era to
another. The small Etruscan and Umbrian core,
encircling the very top of the hill, is surrounded by
Roman remains, beyond which a medieval gate is
evidence of the power Todi had attained by the
thirteenth century, when the building of its extraordinary palaces and churches began. Todi was known
as Tutere when it was the only Etruscan city east of the

Tiber, but was called Tuder by the time the Romans
built the amphitheater, the forum, and the enormous
Augustan arches of a temple or marketplace that
survive today in fragmentary form. The city was
considered so militarily ferocious in these early centuries
that it was sometimes even referred to as Marzia, after
its deity, Mars. Even so, the remoteness of the city from
the Via Flaminia kept Hannibal from invading it,
just as its strategically secure site later spared it the
devastation of Totila and Frederick II.

To provide drinking water, the emperor Trajan
ordered the construction of a complicated network of
cisterns—a feat of hydraulic engineering that was
augmented in medieval times with the addition of still-
visible wells and then forgotten. Recently, however, the
accumulation of water began to threaten the city with
slides and cave-ins, and emergency action has been
taken to drain the subsoil and stabilize the hill.

Today Todi remains much as it was during the
period when, as a free commune, it often sided with
Perugia in the protracted warfare between the Guelphs
and Ghibellines, and was powerful enough to have
taken the neighboring cities of Terni and Amelia under
its own protection. The highest piazza in Umbria, and

Piazza del Capitano del Populo and Piazza dei Priori, Todi one of the most beautiful in all of Italy, lies open at the top of the hill, a great rectangle that is one of the few level spaces in an otherwise steeply canted place. Where the Romans built their forum, medieval Umbrians took stone, marble, and brick to create an elegant piazza that expresses all the conflicts of the age. The towered Duomo, which stands alone at one end, challenges the three medieval civic palaces that anchor the far side of the square, Church and State in stern confrontation. The horizontal sweep of the Duomo's broad stair arrives at a balanced façade that is a careful composition of portals and rose windows, with an intricately carved arch framing the great central door.

Arrayed at the other end of the square, aggressively self-assured and proud, stand the three government palazzi that define its eastern edges: the Lombard Palazzo del Popolo, which is connected by a dramatic staircase to the Gothic Palazzo del Capitano del Popolo, and the severe merloned Palazzo dei Priori. The elegant façade of the double building is rich with subtle rhythms and cadences that are like chamber music played in stone. Trills of trefoiled Gothic windows play against piers in the ground-floor loggia, while the syncopation of connecting gables is a counterpoint to the steady beat of arched windows and dark vaulted openings below. The daring staircase that links the two palazzi cuts dramatically across them, edges sharp as dragon's scales. Its sheer upward thrust to a platform where bishops and *condottieri* once addressed the populace is powerful and bold, and only in descent does a subtle hint of menace intrude, for the sheer drop of the stairs falling away is quick and steep and offers no boundary to its blade-thin edge. Next to it, austere façade thrust upward in challenge, stands the Palazzo dei Priori, where the town magistrate lives, its medieval severity lightened by Pope Leo X's addition of Renaissance windows.

In the adjacent square, a cypress, planted to commemorate the visit of Garibaldi in 1849, towers over a massive Renaissance palazzo that first belonged to the Atti family, whose bloody intrigues recall those at Perugia. The history of the feuds between the Guelph Atti and Ghibelline Chiaravalle was laced with poisonings, brutality, and fratricidal massacres. Todi knew a brief interlude of peace when Pope Paul II compelled the Ghibellines to sell their land and castles, but after he died the conflict was again unleashed, as the Atti, with thirty thousand soldiers, moved against Altobello Chiaravalle. Cornered and set upon by frenzied citizens, he was hacked limb from limb, while one foul old woman, according to legend, seized his naked heart and gulped it down.

Today the women of Todi may be seen washing clothes in the Fonte Scarnabecco, built in 1241 for the horses of the town, and the medieval Porta Marzia built of Roman stones is topped with an elegant loggia that now serves as a private terrace. In the medieval quarter with its toast-colored houses, the streets climb so sharply that stairs have had to be cut into the pavement, and sudden changes in level open to views of red-roofed farmhouses in the valley below, where bright poppies and acacias flower in the spring. With its many levels, its twistings and turnings, Todi is a city of stairs, what Bernard Rudofsky, a noted architect and critic, calls "the leaven in the architectural dough," a ceremonial invitation to the exploration of space. People use these ramps not merely for climbing. They sit on the steps of the Duomo at all hours, talking and watching the activities in the piazza at its feet. The Church of San Fortunato, set high above the street, is reached by zigzag paths and broad tiers of stone steps, like those of the Cathedral, set within neatly clipped and manicured hedges. Its façade is unfinished; raw, weathered bricks divide the upper from the lower part, whose arched central door is framed by clusters of spiral columns, with carvings of vines and human forms whose richness and vigor are reminiscent of the magnificent portal at Orvieto. The interior is high and unexpectedly luminous, with Gothic arches and vaulting supported by clusters of slender columns soaring upward from their high bases. Dark wood choir stalls carved by Antonio Maffei da Gubbio and a wistful fresco by Masolino da Panicale are the most notable works of art in this church, but its primary distinction is a monument to Jacopone da Todi, whose bones are kept in the crypt below.

Born soon after St. Francis died and thirty years before the birth of Dante, Jacopone had been a hedonist until the death of his wife led to his conversion, through the discovery that under her finery she wore a hair shirt, the symbol of self-mortification. From that day Jacopone withdrew from the world, as if crazed by his memories of a luxurious life. He took the vows of a Franciscan tertiary, a member of the lay order that preached and performed charitable deeds. For the next ten years, before he was accepted into the Franciscan Brothers Minor, he walked throughout Umbria and the Marches dressed in a simple robe, preaching, studying, and composing his *laude,* or hymns of praise. By the time of his death, after he had become one of the *fratelli,*

Housefront with Vespa

the reformist Franciscans who were outspoken opponents of the corruption of the papacy, Jacopone had written 211 of his religious hymns and was considered one of the great Franciscan poets. In some of the *laude*, the language was extremely biting, as in his denunciation of Pope Boniface VII:

> *Blasphemous tongue that has poisoned the world,*
> *There is no kind of ugly sin*
> *In which you have not become infamous.*

These stinging words invited the enmity of the Pope, who excommunicated and imprisoned Jacopone; he remained in jail for five years, until Boniface's successor let him go. All the while, Jacopone continued composing his *laude*, which combined Umbrian mysticism and language like that of St. Francis, with its direct appeal to the senses mixed with the aggressive vocabulary of the *battuti*, or flagellants.

A narrow street at the side of San Fortunato passes the cloisters of what was once a convent and is now a school, to arrive at the Rocca on the colossal embankment where the Romans built their temple dedicated to Jupiter. Now children play in the grassy park by the old city walls, and only fragments remain of the cylindrical stone tower of the medieval fortress. It was originally built just before the return of the Popes from Avignon. In 1382 the people of Todi tore it down, only to see it restored by the Perugian *condottiere* Braccio Fortebraccio, but it was permanently destroyed in 1503. Today the quiet green site offers a view of hills wooded with oaks, below which the silvery ribbon of the Tiber winds through neatly cultivated fields bordered by poplars, with the great domed form of Santa Maria della Consolazione rising in the foreground.

Begun in 1508 and completed ninety-five years later, the church stands alone in a grassy meadow just outside the medieval walls—an elegant and serene Renaissance structure that is all white inside and out, a pure evocation of the classical order. Its dome can be seen across the wide Umbrian valley, crowning the structure thought to have been designed by Bramante and built by various architects including Cola da Caprarola. At the time of its construction, undisciplined troops of German foot soldiers wandered up and down the peninsula, looting as they went, and bringing intense suffering to all of Umbria. A chronicler of the time wrote how in Todi and the surrounding district, at night, "many people could be heard crying 'Misery' and people fell dead in the streets and in their houses." Famine took the lives of two-thirds of the population, and people lived on grass and roots for want of bread;

but even under these conditions the building of the church went on.

Near the church, the tree-planted promenade by the medieval gate becomes a small marketplace on Saturdays, as it did in medieval times, when the territory produced an abundance of grain, wine, oil, and fruit. Benvenuto Cellini referred in his autobiography to the counsel of his doctor to drink the wine of Todi to cure an illness. Fifteen hundred years earlier, Pliny wrote of his enjoyment of the town's wine, which he referred to as "Greek," perhaps in reference to the vines the Etruscans brought from Magna Graecia, the Greek cities of southern Italy. The people of the countryside still climb the narrow, winding street to reach the piazza, which is crowded every Saturday for the market. A procession thick with shoppers edges down the Via Mazzini, which curves past the small theater and shops tucked into medieval houses and funnels into the squares. On market day it is jammed with tables and stalls. Women cast careful eyes over the merchandise, while men collect in knots to talk, and teenagers walk in neighboring piazze, loitering in a city where every prospect pleases. Beneath the staircase of the Palazzo Comunale or del Popolo, the man at the *porchetta* stand carves off slices of succulent pork, a tasty Umbrian specialty; the meat comes from pigs fed on acorns of the region, and is seasoned with herbs and roasted on a huge spit.

The town and its surroundings have retained their ancient agricultural character, although tractors have almost completely replaced the white oxen, and tobacco has been substituted to some degree for wheat. Today some of the farmhouses have been elegantly restored and belong to artists, foreigners, or to residents of Rome who use them for weekend villas. Once a year Todi overflows with visitors from all of Italy when it plays host to the national Antiques Fair, which fills an ancient palazzo. But day by day and year by year, the people of the countryside still thread their way through the three gates in the city walls and climb the streets to the breathtaking piazza at the top of the hill.

Street and doorfront, Todi

Stairway to Via Fontesecca, Spoleto

Spoleto

After lunch we walked out to see the lions of Spoleto, and found our way up a steep and narrow street that led us to the city gate, at which, it is traditionally said, Hannibal sought to force an entrance, after the battle of Thrasymene, and was repulsed.

NATHANIEL HAWTHORNE
French and Italian Notebooks

Set against the contours of a wooded hill, the soft gray city of Spoleto is cooled by breezes from the thick forests of Monte Luco, whose two-thousand-foot slopes rise at its back across a narrow gorge of the Tessino River. It is divided between an upper and lower town, and within its dense medieval center, shadowed streets and dark passages alternate with sudden open spaces, small splashes of green in filmy trees and hidden gardens and in the vivid umbrellas of outdoor cafés.

The pentimento of layers of human history reaches back to Neolithic relics, an ancient necropolis, and to the remains of the giant polygonal stones used by the ancient Umbrian inhabitants to fortify the top of the hill. The ruins underlying the medieval building go back to a period four centuries before it became a Roman colony in 241 B.C., long before the mother of the emperor Vespasian built a handsome house that remains preserved beneath the city streets.

In the lower town, blocks of stone that predate the Iron Age form the base of a fourteenth-century tower; others from the first century B.C. support the Torre dell'Olio, so called because of the boiling oil that

was poured down on would-be assailants. Near the massive Palazzo Pompili stands the Porta Fuga, whose name commemorates the place where Hannibal was turned away in 217 B.C. after his stunning victory at Lake Trasimeno brought him to Spoleto in search of further triumphs. The city bears numerous reminders of Rome's gratitude for its loyalty in a wealth of baths, theaters, basilicas, houses, and triumphal arches, as well as in the arched bridge built by Augustus when he changed the course of the Via Flaminia to continue by Spoleto, and in the harmonious flow of city squares as they link easily across the hilly terrain.

Totila the Goth pillaged Spoleto in 546 and built his fortress of stones from the Roman amphitheater. The Lombards, who made Spoleto the capital of a dukedom in the late sixth century, used Roman columns and capitals to build San Salvatore, one of the oldest churches in Umbria, not long after Constantine granted Christians freedom of worship, and its Roman-style basilica is still luminous with Byzantine ornament and early Christian motifs. The thick knotting of time is especially visible in the Piazza del Mercato, which was once the Roman forum, where the city's most important ceremonies took place. Today it is a marketplace where, among mounds of fresh vegetables and fruits, you may find green beans fine as babies' fingers, a golden blaze of zucchini flowers, and trout and perch lying in cool beds of ice. At one end stands a splashing baroque fountain, and at the other, the travertine arch of Drusus, built by the Senate in honor of Tiberius's son. The triumphal arch originally stood more than thirty feet high but lost some of its monumentality when medieval builders raised the level of the town. Excavations have disclosed the remains of an enormous Roman temple that is now part of the crypt of the nearby Church of Sant' Ansano, which is decorated with Romanesque frescoes.

Medieval streets lined with Renaissance and baroque palaces slice into the Piazza del Mercato from every angle—some of them so narrow that only a tiny Fiat 500 can navigate their straits, others dark under Piranesi-like vaulted and tunneled passageways. The Piazza della Libertà, now a busy square, was originally the private courtyard of a seventeenth-century palazzo, which was itself partly built on the remains of a Roman theater. On summer evenings tables, chairs, and potted plants from surrounding restaurants are moved into the street, transforming the square into one big outdoor café that vibrates with the hum of dozens of conversations. And during the Festival of the Two Worlds, Spoleto becomes the setting for music, drama, and ballet. Artisans revive the practice of selling fine crafts and antiques across the stone counters of medieval shops. The music of rehearsing pianists, flutists, and string quartets floats in and out of Renaissance windows above the narrow streets, and throngs of visitors move along the Via Aurelio Saffi, between the Archbishop's Palace and the Palazzo Comunale, to the top of a street that is really a slow, sculpted drop of stairs into the flat piazza in front of the Duomo. Here, chamber orchestras and string quartets perform, and chic visitors drink Campari and eat *strangozzi,* the pasta that is a Spoletan specialty. After they have gone, the Piazza is reclaimed by the city's inhabitants, who stroll through it while their children play hide-and-seek among the columns of the Cathedral portico or fly model planes in the great open space.

The original Duomo fell victim to the struggles between Pope and Emperor, and in 1155 it was destroyed by Frederick Barbarossa, who arrived demanding a payment of tribute. The terrified citizens fled to the slopes of Monte Luco while his troops sacked and burned the town; but forty-three years later, Pope Innocent III consecrated a rebuilt Cathedral with its rose windows wheeling across the simple façade and the Campanile made of travertine scavenged from fallen Roman buildings. Inside the Cathedral are frescoes by Pinturicchio, including one of the Madonna and Child showing Lake Trasimeno transported to the countryside outside Jerusalem, and others by Fra Filippo Lippi, portraying the life of the Virgin. His model was the beautiful nun who had become his mistress. He died before the cycle could be completed, poisoned by a jealous woman, according to Vasari. The Medici wanted to take his body back to Florence, but the Spoletans refused, pleading to keep the remains since they lacked both famous men and ornaments to do them honor. Lorenzo de' Medici assented and sent Filippo Lippi's son, Filippino Lippi, to build the white and gold monument in which the monk's remains still rest.

On one side of the piazza, next to the Baptistery with its octagonal cupola, is the small, elegant Caio Theater, originally built in the seventeenth century. It is the oldest theater in a city now dotted with spaces for performing. Nearby, the severe façade of Sant' Eufemia, tucked unobtrusively into the courtyard of the Archbishop's Palace, hides a chaste and luminous interior. Slender vertical columns rise toward the matrons' gallery upstairs, the only such seating space for women in Umbria—an early feminist was St. Euphemia— while below stands a marble altar decorated with spiraling Cosmatesque designs, and a fine Sienese triptych.

Other churches, dating to early Christian, Lombard, and Romanesque times, rise just beyond the city walls. Of these one of the most notable is the Church of San Pietro, encircled by cypresses above the Via Flaminia. Originally built in the fifth century, on the site of an Iron Age necropolis, to hold a relic of the chains of St. Peter, it was enlarged and rebuilt in the twelfth century, at about the same time as the Duomo, and was given an extremely lively façade in which a stone zoo of beasts, grotesques, and mythological animals is intertwined with foliage and rich abstract designs. In one carved narrative, St. Peter raps the devil on the head with a key as he tries to cheat justice while tipping the scales; in others, a wolf pretends to be reading a book while keeping an eye on a nearby sheep, or plays dead, luring crows to the bait he offers. The exuberant vignettes are vivid illustrations of wrongdoing and punishment, while more naturalistic bas-reliefs deal with people's daily labors. Together they form a captivating image of medieval life, with its

We passed on day after day, until we came to Spoleto, I think the most romantic city I ever saw.... I never saw a more impressive picture, in which the shapes of nature are of the grandest order, but over which the creations of man, sublime from their antiquity and greatness, seem to predominate.

PERCY BYSSHE SHELLEY
"Letter to Thomas Peacock, 1818"

Duomo, Spoleto

extremes of sin and damnation and the consolations of immortality.

Standing on the shoulder of the hill, twelve hundred feet above sea level, is the giant six-towered Rocca, which was constructed by Gattapone of stones from an earlier fortress. Built to strengthen the hold of the papacy after almost a century in Avignon, its occupants at various times included Cardinal Albornoz, several popes, and Lucrezia Borgia, whose father, Pope Alexander VI, in 1498 made her governor of Spoleto. Encircled by a great wall that incorporates some polygonal stones from Umbrian times, this monument to power is now a prison whose massive form frames the upper reaches of the city.

Facing the Rocca above the valley of the Tessino is the Ponte delle Torri, a powerful aqueduct whose ten dramatic brick arches rise 240 feet above the bottom of the gorge and support a span more than 700 feet across. It still carries water to the city from the slopes of Monte Luco. Densely forested with ilex and evergreen oaks, this great hill has had sacred associations since Umbrian times, when local deities were worshiped here. Respecting the tradition, the Romans protected its forests under a special law that prohibited the cutting of sacred trees. In the fourth century it became a Christian refuge when a Syrian disciple of St. Paul established a hermitage, and in the sixth century another Syrian, St. Isaac, became the founder of Monte Luco's first monastery, with a nucleus of Christians fleeing persecution in the East. In the thirteenth century St. Francis and his followers hollowed out a small sanctuary in the rock; two centuries later St. Bernardino expanded it, and it is used to this day by a small group of Capuchin brothers. St. Anthony of Padua and St. Benedict prayed on the mountainside, which is still honeycombed with grottoes and sacred cells. Today hotels and cafés have joined the sanctuaries in these woods as a secular refuge from the steamy heat of summer. Sheep are pastured on its slopes, and black truffles, regarded as a particular delicacy since Roman times, are unearthed from its soil. Lignite mines once produced as much as fifteen million tons a year, and although the seams remain, the mines are now closed.

Michel de Montaigne referred to Spoleto as a "celebrated and commodious town" when he visited Italy in 1580, hoping to find a cure for the gallstones that were causing him pain. In his travels he complained of the lack of "glass or even linen windows" and was offended by the roofs of hollow tiles. Two centuries later, Goethe passed through Spoleto on his way to Rome and praised the aqueduct, which he took to be Roman. Joseph Addison noted in his *Remarks on Several Parts of Italy,* written in 1701–03, that the aqueduct was Gothic, and when James Fenimore Cooper arrived, in 1828, he had the facts straight and referred to it as a structure "that is called Roman and has arches of the Gothic school."

The poet Shelley came to Italy in 1818 with his wife, Mary, the author of *Frankenstein,* and a household that also included, briefly, Byron's illegitimate daughter and her mother, Claire Clairmont. Spoleto impressed Shelley greatly, but he was troubled by the chasm between the natural beauty of Italy and the squalor and poverty of its inhabitants.

By the time Violet Paget settled in Florence in the 1870s, Italy was a unified country. Taking the nom de plume of Vernon Lee, she proceeded to write a series of essays on Italy that combine erudition with a lively evocation of place. Her trip to Spoleto was the prelude to an exploration of Monte Luco and its hermitages. Hans Christian Andersen, on the other hand, wrote of "that peaceful town Spoleto; where the fire burned so brightly in the chimneys; where the music sounded so sweetly from the street; where the people rejoiced outside the church"—and saw the hill towns as sphinx-like presences, rich with mystery and unanswered questions.

In 1958 the composer Gian Carlo Menotti initiated the Festival of the Two Worlds, whose cosmopolitan brilliance bursts upon the scene every summer. After it, when the town ceases to be a romantic backdrop for flute, horn, and human voice, for theater and ballet, it settles back into a slower cadence as a cluster of towers and palazzi set between the deep green of Monte Luco and one of the gentlest valleys of Umbria.

Piazza del Mercato, Spoleto

Women at window, Gubbio

Gubbio

Shelved against the slopes of Monte Ingino, Gubbio looks almost precisely as it did during the Middle Ages, when its bristling towers, steeply vertical buildings, and monumental town hall were the setting of a vigorous city republic. It sits in isolation in the steep wooded hill country to the north of Perugia, terraced and clinging to a precipitous, clifflike site. Although Gubbio is one of Umbria's most ancient cities, it was originally settled at the foot of the hill; Totila and later barbarian invaders were responsible for the vertical form of the town, which was moved up the slope in the early Middle Ages after suffering two devastating attacks in the plain.

The city is dominated by the Palazzo dei Consoli, its square battlements and campanile unmistakable proclamations of civic power. Rising on massive arches that march diagonally up the steep hillside, the palazzo commands attention with its forceful flourish of architectural self-confidence. It opens onto a large, empty piazza with a high parapet that looks far over the mosaic of roofs to the green plain stretching beyond and marks the clear division between the upper and lower town. When Gattapone built it as one of the most beautiful government palazzi in Italy, he tempered its massive form with grace: light touches mark its elegant staircase, delicate third-floor loggia, and finely crenellated tower. Across from it stands the Palazzo Pretorio, and set behind it is the Palazzo Ranghiasci-Brancaleoni with its ripple of iron balconies and many-shuttered windows.

Inside the town hall are the famous Iguvine (or Eugubine) Tablets of varying dates, from the first to the third century B.C. They contain clues to Gubbio's Umbrian past, when it was an important sacred center with many temples and sanctuaries, and make clear the diffusion of Etruscan culture in Umbria. They are the chief extant examples of the Umbrian language. The later Latin-alphabet inscriptions describe the sacrifice of animals before the city gates, as well as priestly rites and ceremonies choreographed with highly detailed precision, and are indications of early religious rituals absorbed and practiced by the Romans. The pine-covered mountains nearby, rising to an altitude of five thousand feet or more, were associated with the Apennine Jove, and were the object of pilgrimages from all over the countryside. There is debate whether the name Gubbio dates from this time or from the Roman era, when the city was known as Iguvium. Roman sarcophagi, coins, and inscriptions in the building's great hall come from the period when Gubbio was a strategic military post on the Via Flaminia. Its isolated site made it a vital link in the chain of communication between Rome and Ravenna, and it flourished during the early years of the empire. An amphitheater, built perhaps during the wars between Pompey and Caesar, and enlarged when Augustus was emperor, now sits like a weathered shell in the soft green of the fields below the town, where its grassy banks of seats are still occupied during summertime theatrical performances.

The mammoth hall of the Palazzo dei Consoli reflects the communal grandeur of medieval days, when Frederick Barbarossa released Gubbio from allegiance to the Holy Roman Empire and allowed power to pass to the Consuls. These representatives of the people met for consultation with the leading families of the city in the Salone dell'Arenga, an imposing vaulted space whose awesome scale was intended to reflect their prestige. While Gubbio flourished, it became the center for the manufacture of ceramics, as artisans perfected the form and ornament of the majolica, black bucchero, and lusterware for which the town is famous. Numerous open doorways on the street outside the Palazzo dei Consoli display ceramics from local workshops, as does the doorframe of the Palazzo del Bargello at the street's end, where they are the only bright touch in an otherwise solemn façade.

In the courtyard of the Palazzo del Bargello is a fountain, known for centuries as the "Fountain of the Mad," of which it is said that anyone who takes three turns around it automatically becomes a citizen of Gubbio. Once a year (on May 15), Gubbio itself gives way to a collective expression of madness and hysterical abandon, at the Corsa dei Ceri, or Race of the Candles, a singular ceremony whose origins are obscure, although it may be connected with a victory, in the twelfth century, over the eleven cities of a league headed by Perugia. The Ceri are three huge wooden forms weighing as much as half a ton each that look more like enormous hourglasses than candlesticks. Each is connected with a particular neighborhood and trade of the city and is surmounted by the image of a saint, one of whom is Gubbio's patron, St. Ubaldo.

It was he who, as Bishop of Gubbio, saved the town from the depredations of the eleven neighboring cities, and his sanctuary on the upper slopes of Monte Ingino is the ultimate destination of three rival teams of twelve colorfully dressed young men who take part in the Corsa. Singing, banqueting, parades, and religious processions precede their mad dash through the city streets, with the monumental burdens carried vertically. Since there is no way for the teams to run abreast through the narrow, winding course, this is not exactly a race; and in any event, the team with the image of

With half of a word's permission, I should fix here for life. The air is so pure, the language so pleasing, the place so inviting.

MRS. PIOZZI
Glimpses of Italian Society in the Eighteenth Century

St. Ubaldo always arrives first at its destination, where it is whirled around three times, and then taken into the cream-colored church where the body of the saint is exhibited and where the Ceri remain until the next year's festival. There are no winners or prizes other than the release of cathartic and explosive energies with which the entire city celebrates the event.

Along the route, in some of the houses lining the streets, may be seen what are known as the *porte dei morti,* or the doors of the dead, set a few feet above the level of the street. According to some accounts, these tall, narrow doors were intended solely for removing the coffins of the deceased, and after the funeral the opening was bricked up to prevent the return of evil spirits. A less romantic and perhaps more convincing explanation is that these openings were actually used as entranceways by means of ladders in dangerous times, and thus served as protection against marauding armies and intruders, while the wider doors at street level were entrances to shops beneath family living quarters. Whatever the truth may be, they give the tightly contained streets of Gubbio what Guido Piovene describes as a somber monochromatic aspect, "profound, spent, the color of the dead," and accentuate the feeling of ghostly silence.

Beyond the streets rises the Palazzo Ducale, where both Charlemagne and Frederick Barbarossa were entertained before it was transformed by Federigo da Montefeltro, ducal ruler of Urbino, who became Gubbio's protector as its days of independence drew to a close. The palace was rebuilt in 1476 and improved upon by his son Guidobaldo, at whose court Castiglione set the scene for *The Courtier.* It was certainly built to resemble the Ducal Palace in Urbino, one of the most cultivated courts in Renaissance Italy, and its inner court has the same gracefully proportioned columns, harmonious colors, and serene ambience, although on a much smaller and simpler scale.

Across the small, shared piazza stands the Duomo, the only cathedral in all of Umbria built at such a distance from the center of town that it seems to have fled from the massive secular statement of power below. The single nave of its somber interior is covered by rows of Gothic arches that support its wooden roof, but it is almost the only church in Gubbio without frescoes by Ottaviano Nelli, the most famous of the city's painters. He inherited a tradition founded by Oderisi, whom Dante called "the honor of Gubbio." The octagonal Gothic Church of San Francesco contains a series of Nelli's frescoes on the life of the Madonna with a likeness of the painter as St. Matthew, while Santa Maria

Castello di Petrioa, between Assisi and Gubbio

Nuova's *Madonna* portrays the Virgin surrounded by saints, musical angels, and two smug, sumptuously dressed donors of the work.

At the bottom of the hill, the old Weavers' Gallery is now a marketplace in which green, gold, and red vegetables spill under the stone arcades where wool and skins were dyed and spread out to dry in the medieval past. The little river Camignano that glides under its arches and flows toward the church was once used by the dyers of cloth, but now it simply bubbles under tiny stone bridges, frequently overflowing its banks in the winter. Streets that climb from the Piazza Quaranta Martiri next to it, named in honor of forty hostages shot by the Germans during World War II, are among the most appealing to wander. The Via Galeotti cuts horizontally across the hill, while the vertical lanes of Via Piccardi and Via Baldassini rise and fall with the steep cant of the land. Their stony gray walls are softened by the color in a pot of hydrangeas or a wisp of olive tree, and by a splash of sunlight slicing through an overhead arch.

Today quiet has once again settled over Gubbio, and the city seems frozen in its medieval aspect. Though its cool gray towers still poke aggressively into the sky, the city is withdrawn and detached, a bit removed from the turmoil of modern life. From the third-floor loggia of the Palazzo dei Consoli it is still easy to imagine soldiers departing for the Crusades or flying down the steep cobbled streets to

take on the Perugians. As we walk the imposing brick road beneath the arches that support the Piazza dei Signori, it seems entirely possible that bishops in full regalia or artisans carrying their Etruscan-inspired ceramics might still appear around the next bend. Once Gubbio was prosperous and commanded a population of fifty thousand; today its clumps of defiant towers and stark silent palazzi still physically command the hillside.

Few travelers came to Gubbio over the centuries because it lay so far from the usual carriage routes. John Addington Symonds spent some time here, and although he regretted the changes in the streets brought about by poor people who had taken residence in what had been the palaces of noblemen, he enjoyed a dinner at which wine was served "after the antique Italian fashion" in stoppered phials of glass, and found it "like sitting down to supper at Emmaus, in some picture of Gian Bellini or of Masolino."

Today all that interrupts the solemn ancient face of the town is the modern imposition of one-way streets and the open skylift that carries visitors to the mountain basilica where Gubbio's patron saint is buried. Restaurants are set within thirteenth- and fourteenth-century buildings, a hotel is made of a Carthusian monastery, and the proud, assertive Gubbio of another day is evoked by its aristocratic palaces and dignified structures that define the city's grandeur in its isolated setting against the Umbrian hills.

Assisi

PAGE NUMBERS IN ITALIC INDICATE PHOTOGRAPHS.

A

Acton, Harold, 20
Addison, Joseph, 16, 67, 106
Alberti, Leon Battista, 31, 47-48, 73
Albornoz, Cardinal, 14, 15, 79, 91, 106
Ammanati, 54
Andersen, Hans Christian, 106
Angelico, Fra (Giovanni da Fiesole), 58, 91
Arezzo, 6, 61-64
    Duomo in, 64
    history of, 61-62
    Joust of the Saracen in, 63
    Museo Archeologico of, 61
    Piazza Grande in, 63
    Pieve of Santa Maria in, 62-63
Arezzo, Guido d', 62
Arezzo, Margaritone d', 45
Assisi, 11, 14, 69, 79-80, 83, 86
    Basilica of St. Francis in, 78, 79-80, 81
    Duomo of San Rufino in, 82, 83, 86
    hermitage of the Carceri in, 83
    religious festivals in, 86
    Rocca in, 79, 87
    San Damiano chapel in, 80
Auden, W. H., 16
Augustus (Octavian), 6, 74, 103

B

Baglioni family, 15, 76
Bartolo, Taddeo di, 33, 38, 45, 53

Beccafumi, Domenico, 33, 34
Belisarius, 7, 22
Benedict, Saint, 7, 25, 106
Berenson, Bernard, 26, 33, 34, 62, 70
Bernardino, Saint, 34-35, 76, 106
Bernini, Giovanni Lorenzo, 34
Bonfigli, Benedetto, 75
Borgia, Rodrigo, 48
Boswell, James, 35
Botticelli, Sandro, 26
Bramante, 101
Brunelleschi, Filippo, 26
Buonconvento, 25
Byzantium, 8

C

Cambio, Arnolfo di, 22, 24, 26
Caprarola, Cola da, 101
Caravaggio, Michelangelo da, 45
Castiglione, Giovanni Benedetto, 110
Catherine, Saint, 14, 34-35
Cellini, Benvenuto, 61, 101
Charlemagne, 8, 110
Charles V, Emperor, 15
Chianti region, 23-24
Chiusi, 3, 6, 22
Cimabue, Giovanni, 80
cities, 8, 10-12, 14-16
    as communes, 11
    constitutional governments in, 12

    inns and food in, 15-16
    life in, 15
    as refuge, 8, 10
    rise of tyranny in, 12, 14
    rivalry among, 11-12
    travelers to, 16
    visual effect of, 15
Città di Bagnorégio, 66, 69
Colle di Val d'Elsa, 24
Colline Metallifere, 3, 23
Constantine the Great, 7, 8, 62, 69, 70, 103
Cooper, James Fenimore, 106
Corot, 55
Cortona, 6, 57-59
    Diocesan Museum in, 58
    history of, 57
    Palazzo Pretorio in, 58
    Piazza della Repubblica in, 57-58
    Piazza Signorelli in, 58
    Santa Margherita Church in, 59
    Santa Maria del Calcinaio Church in, 59
    streets of, 58
Cosimo I, grand duke of Tuscany, 15, 20, 35, 62

D

D'Annunzio, Gabriele, 54, 86, 95
Dante Alighieri, 20, 25, 30, 38, 62, 111
Dennis, George, 54
Dickens, Charles, 16, 30, 35, 43, 64

Diocletian, 7
Dionysius of Halicarnassus, 2
Donatello, 34
Dreiser, Theodore, 77, 86
Duccio di Buoninsegna, 29, 33, 34, 58

E
Etruria, 1-4, 6
Etruscan Places (Lawrence), 52, 54
Etruscans, 2-4, 6
    areas controlled by, 2
    cities built by, 3
    civilization of, 2-3
    cultivation by, 3-4
    geographical origins of, 2
    language of, 2
    religion of, 3
    remnants of, 4, 6
    Roman defeat of, 4, 6
    water controlled by, 3
Evelyn, John, 25

F
Fiesole, 20
Fiesole, Giovanni da (Fra Angelico), 58, 91
Fiesole, Mino da, 53
Fiorentino, Pier Francesco, 110
Fiorentino, Rosso, 53
Florence, 11, 14, 25-26, 29, 37-38, 44, 52
    description of, 20
    Renaissance and, 25-26
    villas surrounding, 26
Forse che Sì, Forse che No (D'Annunzio), 54
Forster, E. M., *v*, 38, 41
Francesca, Piero della, 22, 26, 62, 64
Francis, Saint, 11, 20, 79-80, 106
Franciscan orders, 11-12
Franks, 8, 52
Frederick Barbarossa, Holy Roman emperor, 10-11, 70, 104, 110
Frederick II, 11, 12, 70
Fredi, Bartolo di, 33, 38
Fry, Roger, 53, 94

G
Gamberaia, 26
Gattapone, 106, 109
Ghibellines, 11-12, 24, 29, 30, 37, 52, 62, 76, 91, 97
Ghiberti, Lorenzo, 26, 34
Ghirlandaio, 53
Giotto, 80
Giovanni, Matteo di, 33, 48
Goethe, Johann Wolfgang von, 48, 83, 106
Goths, 3, 7, 22, 52
Gozzoli, Benozzo, 38, 41, 53, 70, 91
Gregory VII, Pope, 22
Gregory IX, Pope, 80
Gregory XI, Pope, 14, 35
Gubbio, 6, 69, 109-11
    Corsa dei Ceri in, 110

Duomo in, 110-11
    Fountain of the Mad in, 110
    history of, 109-10
    Palazzo dei Consoli in, 109-10
    Palazzo Ducale in, 110
    Weavers' Gallery in, 111
Gubbio, Antonio Maffei da, 98
Guelph league, 11-12, 29, 37, 38, 52, 62, 76, 91, 97
Guicciardini, Francesco, 14

H
Hannibal, 6, 20, 103
Hawthorne, Nathaniel, 16, 34, 43, 51, 61, 74, 103
Hazlitt, William, 15
Herodotus, 2
Heurgon, Jacques, 1
Holy Roman Empire, 8, 10-12, 14-15
Howells, William Dean, 16, 34, 65
Huxley, Aldous, 22, 62, 77

I
Innocent III, Pope, 11, 80, 92, 104
I Tatti, 26

J
James, Henry, 16, 30, 34, 37, 41, 42, 45, 54, 55, 59, 64, 73, 77, 86
John, Augustus, 94
Johnson, Samuel, 16
Justinian, 7

L
Landi, Neroccio di Bartolomeo, 33
Landini, Guido, 53
Lanzi, Luigi, 33
Lawrence, D. H., 51, 52, 54, 55, 86
Lippi, Fra Filippo, 45, 104
Liszt, Franz, 35
Livy, 2, 4
Lombards, 3, 8, 22, 52, 103
Lorenzetti, Ambrogio, 29, 31, 33, 35
Lorenzetti, Pietro, 29, 33, 35, 58, 80
Lucca, 15

M
Macaulay, Thomas B., 51, 59
Machiavelli, Niccolò, 44
Maiano, Benedetto da, 38
Maiano, Giuliano da, 38
Maitani, Lorenzo, 89
Manfred, 12
Maremma plain, 4, 23
Margherita, Saint, 59
Maria Nuova, Santa, 111
Martini, Francesco di Giorgio, 33, 59
Martini, Simone, 29, 31, 80
Masaccio, 26
Mathilda, 8

McCarthy, Mary, 12
Medici, Lorenzo de', 14, 22, 55
Medici family, 14-15, 20, 25-26, 57, 64, 104
Memmi, Lippo, 38, 91
Menotti, Gian Carlo, 106
Michelangelo, 34, 41, 62
Michelozzo, 44, 45
Milton, John, 20
Montaigne, Michel Eyquem de, 15, 30, 35, 75, 106
Montalcino, *18*, 25
Montaperti, 30, 37, 44
Monte Amiata, 22, 25, 48
Montefalco, 69, 70
Monte Oliveto Maggiore, 25, 34
Montepulciano, *42*, 43-45
    Bruscello pageant in, 45
    Duomo of, 45
    geographical location of, 43-44
    history of, 43-44
    International Workshop of Music in, 45
    main street of, 44-45
    palazzi of, 44-45
    Palazzo Comunale of, 44
    Piazza Grande of, 44-45
    Pulcinella clock tower in, 44
    San Biagio Church in, 45
    Sant' Agostino Church in, 44
    Vino Nobile of, 43
Mugello valley, 20

N
Nelli, Ottaviano, 110
Norton, Charles Eliot, 89, 92, 94

O
Octavian (Augustus), 6, 74, 103
O'Faoláin, Seán, 32, 34, 58
Olschki, Leonardo, 12
Orvieto, 6, 69, 89, 91-92, 94, *95*
    cliffs of, 92
    Corpus Christi feast in, 91
    Duomo in, *88*, 89, 91, *94*
    history of, 89, 91
    medieval quarter of, 92
    Palazzo del Populo in, 92
    Piazza della Repubblica in, 92
    Well of San Patrizio in, 91

P
Paget, Violet, 106
Palmerucci, Guido, 110, 111
Panicale, Masolino da, 98
Perugia, *viii*, 6, 9, 11, 14, *72*, 73-77, 77
    Corso Vannucci in, 73-74
    history of, 74-76
    Ipogeo dei Volumni in, 74
    Oratory of San Bernardino in, 76
    Palazzo Comunale in, 74
    Quattro Novembre piazza in, 74
    San Michele Arcangelo Church in, 74

San Pietro Church in, 74
    university in, 76-77
Perugino, Il, 70, 77
Peruzzi, 45
Petrarch, 26, 62
Pienza, 46, 47-48, 49
    Duomo in, 48
    Palazzo Comunale in, 48
    Palazzo dei Canonici in, 48
    Palazzo Piccolomini in, 47-48
    Piazza Pio II in, 47
Pietro, Sano di, 33
Pinturicchio, 70, 77, 104
Piovene, Guido, 26, 52, 110
Piranesi, Giambattista, 4
Pisano, Nicola and Giovanni, 33, 34, 74
Pitigliano, 22
Pius II, Pope, 47-48
Plague of 1348, 14, 37, 91
Pliny, 69, 101
Pliny the Younger, 70
Poliziano (Angelo Ambrogini), 45
Poppi, 22
Porsena, Lars, 4, 43

Q
Quercia, Jacopo della, 31, 34, 53

R
Radicofani, 25
Raphael, 76
Redi, Francesco, 43
Ricasoli, Bettino, 23
Robbia, Luccia Della, 35, 41, 45
Roman Empire, 2, 4, 6-7
    civil wars in, 6
    disintegration of, 7
    Etruscans defeated by, 4, 6
    foreign invaders of, 7
    hill town resistance to, 6
    reorganization of, 7
    roads of, 6
Rome, 2, 8, 11
Rossellino, Bernardo, 33, 47-48
Rudofsky, Bernard, 15, 98
Ruskin, John, 16, 35, 94

S
Sabatier, Paul, 80
San Galgano, 25
Sangallo, Antonio da (the Elder), 44, 64, 76, 91
Sangallo, Jacopo, 44
San Gimignano, 12, 37-38, 39-40, 41
    Church of Sant' Agostino in, 41
    Collegiata in, 38, 41
    history of, 37-38
    Palazzo del Popolo in, 36, 38
    St. Fina chapel in, 38
    towers of, 37-38, 41
San Gimignano, Folgore da, 38

Sansepolcro, 22
Sansovino, Andrea, 62
Sant' Antimo, 25
Sassetta, 58
Savonarola, Girolamo, 14, 41
Schorer, Mark, 86
Shelley, Percy Bysshe, 20, 104, 106
Siena, 6, 11, 15, 25, 29-35, 37, 44
    Campo in, 24, 30
    city museum of, 33
    contrade (neighborhoods) of, 31
    Duomo in, 33-34
    Fonte Branda in, 35
    history of, 29-30
    Mangia Tower in, 28, 30
    palazzi in, 32-33
    Palazzo Pubblico in, 30-31
    Palio in, 31-32
    planning of, 30
    San Domenico in, 35
    San Francesco in, 35
    State Archive of, 33
Siena, Barna da, 38
Signorelli, Luca, 25, 26, 53, 58, 70, 91
Sitwell, Osbert, 4, 26
Smollet, Tobias, 15, 77
Sodoma, Il, 25, 33, 35, 45
Sorano, 21, 22
Spello, 6, 69-70
Spoleto, 6, 7, 8, 10, 11, 14, 70, 102, 103-4, 106, 107
    Caio Theater in, 104
    Duomo in, xiv, 104, 105
    Festival of the Two Worlds in, 104, 106
    history of, 103-4
    Monte Luco in, 106
    Ponte delle Torri in, 106
    Rocca in, 106
    San Pietro Church in, 104, 106
    Sant' Eufemia in, 104
Stein, Gertrude, 86
Stendhal, 52
Symonds, John Addington, 16, 43, 45, 62, 76, 80, 89, 92, 111

T
Taine, Hippolyte, 34, 35, 79, 80, 85
Tempietto del Clitunno, 70
Tiber River, 3, 67-68
Todi, 6, 7, 11, 96, 97-98, 101
    Duomo in, 71, 98
    food of, 101
    history of, 97-98
    medieval quarter of, 98
    palazzi in, 98
    piazza in, v, 98
    Rocca in, 101
    San Fortunato Church in, 98
    Santa Maria della Consolazione in, 101
Todi, Jacopone da, 98
Tolomei, Barnardo, 25, 34

Totila, 7, 20, 37, 61, 75, 79, 103, 109
Trasimeno, Lake, 22, 57, 67, 75
travel books, 16
Trease, Geoffrey, 11
Trevelyan, Janet, 8
Trevi, ii, 70
Turner, J. M. W., 92
Tuscany, 19-26
    geography of, 19-23
    language of, 25
    natural resources of, 23
    travelers to, 26

U
Uccello, Paolo, 76
Umbria, 2-4, 6, 67-71
    cities of, 3, 68-71
    deforestation of, 68-69
    geography of, 67-68
    produce of, 69
    as religious center, 7
Umbrians, 2-4, 6
Urban IV, Pope, 12, 91

V
Val d'Arno, 20
Val di Chiana, 4, 22, 25
Val d'Oricia, 48
Vallombrosa, 20
Val Tiberina, 22, 67-69, 73, 97
Vandals, 3, 7
Vanni, Andrea, 35
Vannucci, Pietro, 76
Varro, 3
Vasari, Giorgio, 62, 64
Vecchietta, Lorenzo, 33, 48
Vergil, 2, 57
Via Cassia, 6
Via Flaminia, 6, 68, 103
Via Francigena, 25, 30, 44
Vignola, Giacomo da, 44, 45
Villanovans, 1-2
Volterra, 6, 51-55
    Balze of, 51
    Baptistery of, 53
    Duomo of, 53
    Etruscan Museum in, 54-55
    fortress in, 51, 55
    history of, 52
    location of, 51-52
    Palazzo Pretorio in, 50, 53
    Piazza dei Priori in, 52
    Porta all'Arco in, 52, 53

W
Wharton, Edith, 12, 16, 41, 44, 51
World War II, 22, 26, 41

Street sweeper, Orvieto

All of the color separations for this book were lovingly prepared by the photographer's own hand.

The typefaces used in this book are Adobe Bembo and Monotype Corporation's Bell Gothic Light. The text was composed entirely on a Macintosh system, using QuarkXpress.